# FOLLOW THE MONEY
## HANDBOOK

# FOLLOW THE MONEY
## H A N D B O O K

**LARRY MAKINSON**

CENTER FOR RESPONSIVE POLITICS
WASHINGTON, D.C.

# ACKNOWLEDGEMENTS

The tips and hints contained in this book were gleaned over the years by many people in newsrooms and public records offices across the nation. Deserving particular thanks for their long-term assistance and advice in researching the money trail and digging up the patterns are Kent Cooper of the Federal Election Commission, Josh Goldstein and Ellen Miller of the Center for Responsive Politics, and Howard Weaver of the *Anchorage Daily News*, who first saw the potential of removing one reporter from daily deadlines to begin investigating the sources of money in state elections. Additional (and invaluable) assistance in preparing this book was provided by Center staffers Margaret Engle and Jackie Duobinis. The cover illustration is by John Howard. Cover and layout design are by Peter Deutsch and Beth Russo of Deutsch Design Inc.

This book is dedicated to Philip M. Stern, who started many a reporter down the trail of money in politics.

**The Center for Responsive Politics** is a non-profit, non-partisan research organization based in Washington, D.C. Founded in 1983, the Center specializes in the study of Congress and particularly the role that money plays in its elections and actions. The Center's National Library on Money & Politics provides custom research for news organizations and others, using a computerized database that combines contributor classifications with current and historical federal campaign records. Major funders of the Center include the Arca Foundation, Carnegie Corporation, the Ford Foundation, the Joyce Foundation, the John D. and Catherine T. MacArthur Foundation, the Rockefeller Family Fund and the Florence and John Schumann Foundation. Funding for this book was provided by the Joyce Foundation.

© 1994 by the Center for Responsive Politics
ISBN #0-939715-20-1

# CONTENTS

# FOREWORD

"Follow the Money," the watchword of Watergate, is the hallmark of the work of the Center for Responsive Politics. Since 1988, under the inspired guidance of our Research Director, Larry Makinson, the Center has examined the details and patterns of who's supplying the dollars that fuel America's federal elections, exposing and documenting the influence of major contributors over the federal electoral process, the never-ending quest by candidates to secure campaign cash, the connection between contributions and legislative action (or inaction), and the continually spiraling costs of federal elections.

Over the years, the Center has frequently been asked to help others undertake similar research on state, county and city office-holders. In order to meet these growing requests — both by the media and by nonprofit organizations — the Center launched a formal effort in 1992 to replicate the Center's analytic capabilities. We developed a research prototype designed to follow the money at every level of government. We've taken that prototype on the road, working with hundreds of journalists and activists throughout the country, adapting our research model to their needs. This work has helped bring critically important information about who funds America's political campaigns out of the backrooms of lawmakers and lobbyists and into the living rooms of millions of Americans through their newspapers, radios and televisions.

This *Follow the Money Handbook* is our attempt to take what we have learned in seminars and conferences throughout the country, in one-on-one meetings, and in thousands of telephone conversations and put it in a format that journalists everywhere can use to do their own research. Regard it as a work in progress. We welcome your feedback on what works and what doesn't, and we encourage you to share what you have learned about tracking the money, so that we can pass it along to others in future editions.

Twenty years after the Watergate scandals, public anger over "politics as usual" is higher than it's ever been. In poll after poll, between 75 and 80 percent of the American people say they believe that elected officials care more about special interests than about the people themselves. As long as politicians can continue to accept (and actively solicit) thousands of dollars in contributions every election year from the very industries and interests they're supposed to be regulating — at no political risk to themselves, and without the voters ever being the wiser — the only direction that public cynicism can go is up. The roots of change can be found in the pages of this book.

*Ellen S. Miller*
*Executive Director*
*October 1994*

# WHY FOLLOW THE MONEY?

This handbook is designed specifically for reporters and editors, and is written from the background of nearly 10 years of research into tracking the patterns of money and politics at both the state and national levels. With the tips, guidelines and source materials in this book, any news organization — of any size — can begin systematically tracking campaign contributions to political candidates, delivering to their readers, viewers or listeners a crucially important (yet often unseen) side of modern American politics.

For better or worse, it is a fact of political life that good looks, good ideas and an impressive resumé are not the most important ingredients for political success these days. All too often, money is. Without that most precious of commodities, candidates lack the resources to take their message to the voters. Indeed, candidates without sufficient funds are often seen to lack "credibility" by the PACs, interest groups and even news organizations who are the modern handicappers of political viability.

Wealthy candidates can supply their own — or at least lend themselves the money it takes to get started, in the hopes that their personal loans will be repaid as the money rolls in later. Candidates of more moderate means must seek other people's money to run their campaigns, and this handbook shows how to keep close tabs on exactly where that money comes from.

The importance of tracking the money that politicians use to run their campaigns can hardly be overstated. It influences not only who wins public office, but who is most likely to have first-class access to the candidate after they've moved off the campaign trail and into positions of power.

There's an assumption in everything that follows in this handbook — it's *important* to follow the money. So that no assumptions go unanswered, here are some reasons why.

## THE PHANTOM CAMPAIGN

During every election season, candidates wage two campaigns: the visible campaign — the speeches, door-knocking, print and broadcast ads, brochures and direct mail pieces that advertise the candidate's positions to the voters. This is the campaign that is traditionally covered by news organizations. Unseen by public at large, however, is a second "phantom" campaign that takes place simultaneously. The target of this campaign is not the voters, but the interest groups and wealthy individuals who can supply the money it will take to buy the bumper stickers, brochures and 30-second-spots of the visible campaign. The issues that a candidate talks about in targeting these contributors are often totally different from the issues they talk about to the public. And the people they're pitching are the ones who'll be knocking on their door asking for support once the election is over. Exposing the details of this phantom campaign — and identifying the players — provides a much more fully-rounded picture of the candidate and the positions he or she will take once they attain office.

## UNDERSTANDING GRIDLOCK

Gridlock is a term applied more and more to legislative bodies these days, but it's a mistake to think of it entirely in partisan terms. Much gridlock is indeed due to irreconcilable differences between Republican and Democratic factions within Congress or state legislatures, but much of it has nothing to do with party labels. When two or more competing (and contributing) interests face off over pending legislation, many lawmakers are loathe to disappoint either side. The result is often legislative inaction, or at the very least a substantial lengthening of the legislative process. Major legislative initiatives often take many years — sometimes even decades — to eventually win approval. A big reason is the campaign dollars that wealthy interests have invested in maintaining the status quo and killing legislation that threatens it.

## POLITICS IS A TWO-WAY STREET

The normal give and take of politics takes on an entirely new dimension when serious sums of money enter into the equation. And it's a two-way street. Politicians don't only feel the pressure of interest groups with the power to bestow dollars on their campaign, many politicians are quite aggressive about raising funds from interests whose bottom line is at stake in government decisions. When politicians routinely seek contributions from the industries they regulate — a common practice in Washington and many state capitals — it ought to set off alarm bells in newsrooms (and the homes of taxpayers) across the nation.

## UNCOVERING THE CASH CONSTITUENTS

Political officials typically have two sets of constituents, often with widely divergent interests. First there are their legal constituents — the voters in the city, state or district they represent. But once they attain office, every politician quickly develops a second set of constituents whose interests are linked more to the politician's committee assignments or political authority, rather than the geographic area they represent. These "cash constituents" supply a substantial portion of the dollars it takes to finance the next election campaign, and those dollars are directed often with a very specific political agenda in mind — one which may or may not benefit the home-district constituents or the public at large. Campaign contributions from these cash constituents work double-time if the candidate gets them but the voters never hear about it. The politician knows where the money comes from, and will be mindful of the fact when the contributor, or their lobbyist, comes knocking on the door. The contributor certainly knows where their money went. The only ones left in the dark are the public, unless the reporting of every politician's "cash constituents" becomes a regular part of political reporting.

## BUT IT'S LEGAL . . .

If it were illegal for a business or interest group to give a $1,000 check to a politician one day then arrive at their office looking for legislative favors the next, instances of such "contributions" would be front page news. Under the rules by which our elections are currently played, however, such contributions are not only legal, they are commonplace — even necessary, many would argue, since without them political campaigns as we know them could not be waged. Because they're legal, they rarely wind up on page one — or sometimes anywhere else in our daily newspapers or newscasts. To politicians, contributors and journalists alike, they've become a part of the background noise of modern life. We hardly pay attention any more.

At what cost?

Public distrust of politicians and government could hardly be higher. Complaints that lawmakers have lost touch with the people they are supposed to represent are legion. Politics in general has degenerated from being a participatory sport to a spectator sport, to a sport in which no one any longer even seems to be paying attention, except to complain that it doesn't work.

Follow the money that finances political campaigns and you will discover, however, that some people *are* paying attention. Those with very specific political goals, and the money to back them up, pay close attention indeed to every move made by legislative bodies from the local planning and zoning commission to the halls of Congress. For these cash constituents, contributions to political figures have become simply a cost of doing business. Like investments in the stock market, they can be risky, with no guarantee of success. But combined with some political savvy, and reinforced with increasingly sophisticated lobbying efforts, these investments often pay handsome rewards for those who can afford to ante up.

Introduce your readers, listeners and viewers to these political insiders and the specifics of their game, and you will perform a public service far beyond the routine reporting of political charges, countercharges and public posturing. Beneath the surface of political discourse, a much more interesting and important game is taking place, largely unseen by the public and unreported by news organizations. Follow the money and you will find yourself opening a window on this hidden game — a window that deserves to be pulled wide open for everyone to see.

*Larry Makinson*
*Washington, D.C.*
*October 1994*

**I**

# THE MONEY IN THE SYSTEM

# 1

## THE BIG PICTURE

**E**lections these days are big business. Only in the least populous states for the lowliest offices — and sometimes not even there — can an individual still set out on his or her own with a handshake, a smile and a good reserve of shoe leather, to door-knock and soapbox their way to public office. Many still try, but only a tiny minority are successful. To win a seat in a state legislature, a big city council or the U.S. Congress these days takes not only an attractive candidate, but a good organization and plenty of advertising. And that takes money.

In Washington, D.C. (and on a smaller level in big cities and state capitals around the nation) a cadre of professional consultants has taken root, prospered and multiplied. A decade ago, when I was covering elections in Alaska, candidates for the legislature were not considered serious unless they had hired a professional to help run their campaign — whether through polling, advertising, campaign management, fundraising, or the whole package. Statewide candidates were handicapped as losers if they hadn't brought in someone from out of state — preferably with a national reputation. And this was in 1984, in *Alaska!*

No one today is surprised that it takes a multi-million dollar effort to run a presidential campaign. But in the four decades since the first "I Like Ike" TV commercials hit the air, the business of political advertising and consulting has penetrated to nearly every level of office-seekers. These professionals don't come cheap, so candidates are spending more and more of their campaign time dialing for dollars, and hawking their talents (and their electability) before a never-ending parade of business, labor and ideological groups that can provide campaign cash.

And for good reason. In the 1992 elections, the average winning campaign for the U.S. House of Representatives cost more than half a million dollars. Senate races averaged around $4 million. The least expensive senate victory, in New Hampshire, cost $1.1 million. The most expensive, in New York, cost $15 million.

State legislative races vary widely. The average state house candidate in Montana spent less than $4,000 in 1992. In California, on the other hand, million-dollar state assembly races no longer raise eyebrows.

Where does all the money come from? No comprehensive survey has ever answered that question at the state level, but for the past three election cycles the Center for Responsive Politics in Washington, D.C. has tried to answer it at the federal level, tracking the sources of the hundreds of millions of dollars delivered to congressional and presidential campaigns. The following pages provide a summary of what the Center has found.

In nearly every race, the biggest proportion of campaign funds comes from the combination of political action committees (PACs) and large individual donors. Small contributions (those under $200) typically account for less than 20 percent of the total raised by congressional candidates.

Counting only the dollars that came from PACs and from individual donations of $200 or more, the Center has found that some 80 percent of the total dollars ($295.4 million that we were able to identify) came from business interests. Another $43.3 million came from organized labor, nearly all of it funneled through PACs. And $29.3 million came from ideological and other single-issue interest groups.

One important finding that the Center has made in its research is the consistency with which interest groups contribute. The same players reappear year after year, and while their giving may go up in years when their issue is at the top of the congressional agenda (the health and insurance industries in 1992, for example), they can be counted on as major contributors with great regularity.

The charts on the following pages illustrate the major contributor groups, broken down into 12 main sectors.* The contributions were made during the 1991-92 election cycle.

* The summary is taken from *Open Secrets: The Encyclopedia of Congressional Money and Politics* by Larry Makinson and Joshua Goldstein of the Center for Responsive Politics.

# Agriculture                                                    $24.9 million

*An important player in Washington that has maintained its longtime influence despite the decline of the family farm, agricultural contributors gave nearly $25 million to congressional and presidential candidates in 1991-92. Crop production and processing was the sector's leading source of campaign funds, but it accounted for only one-quarter of the total dollars. The rest came from a wide range of affiliated industries, from food processors and supermarkets to pesticide and fertilizer manufacturers, tobacco companies, dairy farmers, poultry and livestock producers, and the forest products industry.*

|  | Total | From PACs | To Dems | To Repubs |
|---|---|---|---|---|
| Crop Production & Processing | $5,868,649 | 54% | 55% | 45% |
| Tobacco | $2,818,861 | 81% | 53% | 47% |
| Dairy | $2,107,911 | 83% | 63% | 37% |
| Poultry & Livestock | $2,551,679 | 50% | 47% | 53% |
| Agricultural Services/Products | $3,470,020 | 73% | 47% | 53% |
| Food Processing & Sales | $5,108,064 | 57% | 37% | 62% |
| Forest Products | $2,709,343 | 61% | 25% | 75% |
| Other & Unclassified | $257,597 | 0% | 33% | 67% |
| **TOTAL** | **$24,892,124** | **62%** | **46%** | **53%** |

## Top 10 Agricultural Contributors

| Rank | Total | Contributor | Category |
|---|---|---|---|
| 1 | $1,004,848 | RJR Nabisco* | Tobacco/Food |
| 2 | $877,550 | Associated Milk Producers | Dairy |
| 3 | $775,147 | Philip Morris* | Tobacco/Food |
| 4 | $636,120 | US Tobacco* | Tobacco |
| 5 | $531,778 | Food Marketing Institute | Food Stores |
| 6 | $427,470 | National Cattlemen's Assn | Livestock |
| 7 | $345,650 | Archer-Daniels-Midland Corp | Grain Traders |
| 8 | $345,071 | Mid-America Dairymen | Dairy |
| 9 | $313,588 | ConAgra Inc | Food Products |
| 10 | $311,707 | American Sugarbeet Growers Assn | Sugar |

* Contributions came from more than one affiliate or subsidiary

# Communications/Electronics $21.2 million

*The big money here comes from two main sources: the telecommunications industry (primarily local and long distance telephone companies) and the entertainment industry, made up mainly of the TV and motion picture industries. The phone money came predominantly from AT&T and the regional Bell systems. Nearly nine-tenths of that money was delivered through political action committees. The broadcasting and movie money — which tilted heavily toward Democratic candidates — came mostly through individual donors rather than PACs.*

| | Total | From PACs | To Dems | To Repubs |
|---|---|---|---|---|
| Publishing | $3,059,581 | 15% | 55% | 44% |
| Media/Entertainment | $8,018,782 | 32% | 72% | 28% |
| Telephone Utilities | $5,904,399 | 88% | 56% | 43% |
| Telecom Equipment & Services | $909,340 | 49% | 52% | 48% |
| Electronics Mfg & Services | $1,088,233 | 42% | 37% | 63% |
| Computer Equipment & Services | $2,212,954 | 26% | 50% | 49% |
| Other & Unclassified | $39,175 | 1% | 63% | 37% |
| TOTAL | $21,232,464 | 46% | 60% | 40% |

## Top 10 Communications & Electronics Contributors

| Rank | Total | Contributor | Category |
|---|---|---|---|
| 1 | $1,397,883 | AT&T* | Long Distance |
| 2 | $963,353 | BellSouth Corp* | Phone Utilities |
| 3 | $644,249 | National Cable Television Assn | Cable TV |
| 4 | $631,869 | GTE Corp* | Phone Utilities |
| 5 | $583,089 | Time Warner* | Movies/Publish |
| 6 | $562,342 | Ameritech Corp* | Phone Utilities |
| 7 | $522,400 | National Assn of Broadcasters | Entertainment |
| 8 | $432,910 | United Telecommunications* | Phone Utilities |
| 9 | $401,834 | Walt Disney Co* | Movies/Resorts |
| 10 | $331,512 | Pacific Telesis Group | Phone Utilities |

* Contributions came from more than one affiliate or subsidiary

# Construction                                    $15.2 million

General contractors engaged in commercial, industrial, utility and highway construction were the biggest single source of campaign funds within the construction sector. Overall they outspent home builders by nearly three-to-one. Other notable sources of contributions were more specialized subcontractors, engineering and architectural firms, and building materials suppliers. A close partner of the construction industry, often weathering the same economic ups and downs, is the real estate industry, which is included separately in the Finance, Insurance & Real Estate sector, described on page 10.

|  | Total | From PACs | To Dems | To Repubs |
|---|---|---|---|---|
| General Contractors | $6,500,194 | 26% | 42% | 58% |
| Home Builders | $2,216,175 | 59% | 45% | 55% |
| Special Trade Contractors | $1,686,428 | 24% | 38% | 61% |
| Construction Services | $1,974,020 | 33% | 62% | 38% |
| Building Materials | $2,869,672 | 23% | 35% | 64% |
| TOTAL | $15,246,489 | 31% | 43% | 57% |

## Top 10 Construction Contributors

| Rank | Total | Contributor | Category |
|---|---|---|---|
| 1 | $1,074,827 | National Assn of Home Builders* | Resid Constr |
| 2 | $677,899 | Associated General Contractors* | Genl Contractors |
| 3 | $353,558 | Fluor Corp* | Heavy Constr |
| 4 | $203,580 | National Utility Contractors Assn | Utility Constr |
| 5 | $191,877 | Bechtel Corp | Heavy Constr |
| 6 | $184,150 | Associated Builders & Contractors | Builders Assn |
| 7 | $163,500 | National Electrical Contractors Assn | Subcontractors |
| 8 | $161,901 | Sheet Metal/Air Cond Contractors | Subcontractors |
| 9 | $128,703 | CH2M Hill | Engineers |
| 10 | $116,375 | Morrison-Knudsen | Genl Contract |

* Contributions came from more than one affiliate or subsidiary

## Defense                                          $8.3 million

*While every one of the 12 main industry and interest group sectors increased their giving in 1992, total contributions from the defense sector grew the least. That reflects the industry's continuing post-Cold War economic slump. Within the sector, defense aerospace contractors gave about twice as much as defense electronics firms. Overall, nearly 90 percent of the defense industry's contributions came from PACs.*

|  | Total | From PACs | To Dems | To Repubs |
|---|---|---|---|---|
| Defense Aerospace | $4,748,928 | 92% | 55% | 44% |
| Defense Electronics | $2,433,503 | 86% | 56% | 44% |
| Miscellaneous Defense | $1,146,329 | 83% | 53% | 47% |
| TOTAL | $8,328,760 | 89% | 55% | 45% |

### Top 10 Defense Contributors

| Rank | Total | Contributor | Category |
|---|---|---|---|
| 1 | $536,335 | Martin Marietta Corp | Air Defense |
| 2 | $464,055 | General Dynamics | Air Defense |
| 3 | $446,570 | Textron Inc | Air Defense |
| 4 | $377,515 | Northrop Corp | Air Defense |
| 5 | $376,383 | Rockwell International | Air Defense |
| 6 | $371,643 | McDonnell Douglas* | Air Defense |
| 7 | $366,537 | Lockheed Corp | Air Defense |
| 8 | $312,300 | General Atomics | Misc Defense |
| 9 | $311,531 | Chrysler Corp* | Air Defense |
| 10 | $307,100 | Raytheon* | Air Defense |

* Contributions came from more than one affiliate or subsidiary

## Energy & Natural Resources          $21.3 million

*Oil and gas producers supplied the biggest share of campaign dollars from this sector, as they have consistently over the years. In 1991-92 they gave $9.2 million to congressional and presidential candidates. Natural gas pipeline companies added another $2.4 million. The other big givers here were the nation's electric utilities, which doled out nearly $4.6 million — nearly 90 percent of it through PACs.*

|                                      | Total        | From PACs | To Dems | To Repubs |
|--------------------------------------|--------------|-----------|---------|-----------|
| Oil & Gas Production/Marketing       | $9,234,077   | 50%       | 35%     | 65%       |
| Natural Gas Distribution             | $2,393,866   | 76%       | 59%     | 41%       |
| Mining                               | $1,844,760   | 61%       | 38%     | 62%       |
| Electric Utilities                   | $4,555,470   | 87%       | 58%     | 42%       |
| Waste Mgmt/Environmental Svcs        | $1,717,181   | 53%       | 58%     | 42%       |
| Commercial Fishing                   | $314,209     | 35%       | 73%     | 27%       |
| Other & Unclassified                 | $1,281,672   | 79%       | 46%     | 54%       |
| TOTAL                                | $21,341,235  | 63%       | 46%     | 54%       |

## Top 10 Energy & Natural Resources Contributors

| Rank | Total      | Contributor                           | Category           |
|------|------------|---------------------------------------|--------------------|
| 1    | $683,558   | Waste Management Inc*                  | Waste Mgmt         |
| 2    | $627,155   | ACRE (Action Cmte Rural Electric)*    | Rural Electric     |
| 3    | $493,092   | Atlantic Richfield                    | Oil & Gas          |
| 4    | $420,581   | Chevron Corp                          | Oil & Gas          |
| 5    | $397,825   | Coastal Corp*                         | Natural Gas        |
| 6    | $364,541   | Southern Co*                          | Electric Utilities |
| 7    | $358,060   | Exxon Corp                            | Oil & Gas          |
| 8    | $348,250   | Cooper Industries                     | Power Plant Const  |
| 9    | $306,450   | Occidental Petroleum*†                | Oil & Gas          |
| 10   | $298,650   | Southern California Edison            | Electric Utilities |

* Contributions came from more than one affiliate or subsidiary
† Includes only energy-related operations

## Finance, Insurance & Real Estate    $71.1 million

*This is the giant of all the contributor sectors, providing more than $71 million to federal candidates in the 1992 elections. Within the sector, four heavyweight industries provided most of the money— real estate interests gave $16.5 million, the securities & investment industry gave $15.9 million, insurance companies and agents gave $14.9 million and commercial banks passed out $11.2 million to candidates for Congress and the presidency. Two-thirds of the banking and insurance contributions came from political action committees, while three-quarters of the real estate and securities industry money came from individuals.*

|  | Total | From PACs | To Dems | To Repubs |
|---|---|---|---|---|
| Commercial Banks | $11,196,321 | 66% | 52% | 48% |
| Savings & Loans | $1,318,827 | 70% | 53% | 47% |
| Credit Unions | $697,305 | 95% | 65% | 35% |
| Finance/Credit Companies | $1,042,551 | 55% | 51% | 49% |
| Securities & Investment | $15,936,222 | 23% | 60% | 40% |
| Insurance | $14,944,778 | 65% | 50% | 50% |
| Real Estate | $16,472,555 | 24% | 55% | 45% |
| Accountants | $4,877,052 | 51% | 55% | 45% |
| Other & Unclassified | $4,606,265 | 5% | 45% | 54% |
| TOTAL | $71,091,876 | 42% | 54% | 46% |

### Top 10 Finance, Insurance & Real Estate Contributors

| Rank | Total | Contributor | Category |
|---|---|---|---|
| 1 | $2,954,973 | National Assn of Realtors | Real Estate |
| 2 | $1,692,508 | American Bankers Assn* | Comml Banks |
| 3 | $1,544,701 | American Institute of CPA's | Accountants |
| 4 | $1,373,955 | National Assn of Life Underwriters | Life Insurance |
| 5 | $898,545 | Goldman, Sachs & Co | Securities |
| 6 | $881,820 | American Express* | Stocks/Credit |
| 7 | $640,040 | Prudential Insurance* | Insurance |
| 8 | $627,864 | Merrill Lynch* | Securities |
| 9 | $589,798 | Indep Insurance Agents of America | Insurance |
| 10 | $581,880 | American Council of Life Insurance | Life Insurance |

* Contributions came from more than one affiliate or subsidiary

## Health                                   $31.7 million

With a complete overhaul of the nation's health care system looming at the top of the agenda of both Congress and the White House in 1992, the nation's health providers dramatically boosted their political contributions to federal candidates. Physicians and other health professionals led the way, providing more than $21 million in campaign cash to federal candidates. Pharmaceutical companies and health products manufacturers added another $4.4 million, and hospitals and nursing homes gave $3.6 million. The insurance industry, included in the financial sector on the previous page, added nearly $15 million of its own, bringing the combined health & insurance outlay to more than $46 million in the 1992 elections.

|  | Total | From PACs | To Dems | To Repubs |
|---|---|---|---|---|
| Health Professionals | $21,421,791 | 46% | 56% | 44% |
| Hospitals/Nursing Homes | $3,638,760 | 46% | 65% | 35% |
| Health Services | $1,122,272 | 30% | 65% | 35% |
| Pharmaceuticals/Health Products | $4,439,371 | 67% | 47% | 53% |
| Other & Unclassified | $1,088,045 | 0% | 61% | 39% |
| TOTAL | $31,710,239 | 47% | 56% | 43% |

## Top 10 Health Contributors

| Rank | Total | Contributor | Category |
|---|---|---|---|
| 1 | $3,245,544 | American Medical Assn* | Doctors |
| 2 | $1,434,408 | American Dental Assn* | Dentists |
| 3 | $870,227 | American Acad of Ophthalmology | Eye Doctors |
| 4 | $658,596 | American Chiropractic Assn* | Chiropractors |
| 5 | $617,102 | American Hospital Assn* | Hospitals |
| 6 | $401,000 | American Podiatry Assn | Doctors |
| 7 | $398,366 | American Optometric Assn | Eye Doctors |
| 8 | $383,269 | American Health Care Assn | Nursing Homes |
| 9 | $332,925 | Amer College of Emerg Physicians | Doctors |
| 10 | $311,019 | American Nurses Assn | Nurses |

* Contributions came from more than one affiliate or subsidiary

## Lawyers & Lobbyists                    $44.1 million

*When looking at PAC contributions alone, lawyers and lobbyists appear to be a second-tier player among business sectors, but a closer examination of their contributions shows that this is due more to the way they give than to how much they give. Fully 86 percent of the contributions from lawyers and lobbyists came through individual donations, and when added to the PAC dollars, their overall total during 1991-92 rose to more than $44 million — second only to the Finance, Insurance & Real Estate sector. Democrats were the main beneficiaries, capturing nearly three-quarters of the total contributions.*

|  | Total | From PACs | To Dems | To Repubs |
|---|---|---|---|---|
| Lawyers/Law Firms | $38,237,491 | 16% | 73% | 27% |
| Lobbyists/Foreign Agents | $5,821,253 | 5% | 72% | 28% |
| TOTAL | $44,058,744 | 14% | 73% | 27% |

### Top 10 Lawyer & Lobbyist Contributors

| Rank | Total | Contributor | Category |
|---|---|---|---|
| 1 | $2,361,135 | Assn of Trial Lawyers of America | Trial Lawyers |
| 2 | $538,228 | Akin, Gump et al | Law/Lobby |
| 3 | $372,666 | Cassidy & Associates | Lobbyists |
| 4 | $350,566 | Skadden, Arps et al | Law/Lobby |
| 5 | $344,611 | Jones, Day et al | Law/Lobby |
| 6 | $269,264 | Williams & Jensen | Law/Lobby |
| 7 | $250,342 | Verner, Liipfert et al | Law/Lobby |
| 8 | $203,374 | Vinson & Elkins | Law/Lobby |
| 9 | $183,192 | Preston, Gates et al | Law/Lobby |
| 10 | $180,389 | Latham & Watkins | Law/Lobby |

\* Contributions came from more than one affiliate or subsidiary

## Miscellaneous Business　　　　　$38.5 million

This catchall category includes everything from steel makers to beer distributors, restaurants to chemical companies, hotels to advertising agencies. Major contributor groups within the sector include the food & beverage industry ($4 million), chemical manufacturers ($3 million), and a wide collection of business services and manufacturing companies.

| | Total | From PACs | To Dems | To Repubs |
|---|---|---|---|---|
| Business Associations | $934,666 | 70% | 33% | 66% |
| Food & Beverage | $4,064,037 | 46% | 38% | 61% |
| Beer, Wine & Liquor | $4,079,617 | 52% | 56% | 44% |
| Retail Sales | $4,530,113 | 33% | 49% | 51% |
| Miscellaneous Services | $2,174,644 | 24% | 50% | 50% |
| Business Services | $7,502,660 | 10% | 55% | 44% |
| Gambling/Live Entertainment | $1,212,097 | 21% | 67% | 33% |
| Lodging/Tourism | $1,595,139 | 25% | 50% | 49% |
| Chemicals | $3,088,619 | 49% | 31% | 68% |
| Steel Production | $870,603 | 32% | 38% | 62% |
| Misc Manufacturing/Distribution | $8,425,812 | 28% | 41% | 59% |
| **TOTAL** | **$38,478,007** | **32%** | **47%** | **53%** |

### Top 10 Miscellaneous Business Contributors

| Rank | Total | Contributor | Category |
|---|---|---|---|
| 1 | $977,081 | National Beer Wholesalers Assn | Beer Distrib |
| 2 | $571,197 | National Restaurant Assn* | Restaurants |
| 3 | $525,569 | Dow Chemical* | Chemicals |
| 4 | $452,363 | Pepsico* | Soft Drinks/Rest |
| 5 | $368,000 | Stone Container Corp | Paper Packaging |
| 6 | $296,434 | McDonald's Corp | Restaurants |
| 7 | $295,287 | National Fedn of Indep Business | Business Assns |
| 8 | $284,649 | Intl Council of Shopping Centers | Retail Sales |
| 9 | $277,260 | FMC Corp | Chemicals |
| 10 | $267,090 | Coca-Cola Co* | Soft Drinks |

* Contributions came from more than one affiliate or subsidiary

# Transportation                                   $19.0 million

The automotive and air transport industries were the biggest givers within the transportation sector during 1991-92, though within those groups much of the money came not from airlines and auto makers, but from auto dealers and from the nation's two giant delivery services, UPS and Federal Express. The trucking industry, railroads and sea transport companies round out the transportation sector, which gave a combined $19 million in the 1992 elections.

|                        | Total        | From PACs | To Dems | To Repubs |
|------------------------|--------------|-----------|---------|-----------|
| Air Transport/Aerospace | $5,655,211   | 83%       | 56%     | 44%       |
| Automotive             | $6,494,504   | 59%       | 36%     | 64%       |
| Trucking               | $1,821,556   | 56%       | 48%     | 52%       |
| Railroads              | $2,179,996   | 82%       | 48%     | 52%       |
| Sea Transport          | $2,062,351   | 54%       | 54%     | 46%       |
| Miscellaneous Transport | $776,072    | 36%       | 48%     | 51%       |
| TOTAL                  | $18,989,690  | 67%       | 47%     | 53%       |

## Top 10 Transportation Contributors

| Rank | Total | Contributor | Category |
|------|-------|-------------|----------|
| 1 | $1,784,375 | National Auto Dealers Assn | Auto Dealers |
| 2 | $1,472,357 | United Parcel Service | Delivery Svcs |
| 3 | $851,852 | General Electric* | Aerospace |
| 4 | $771,474 | General Motors* | Auto Manuf |
| 5 | $747,445 | Federal Express Corp | Delivery Svcs |
| 6 | $713,390 | Union Pacific Corp* | Railroads |
| 7 | $538,550 | Auto Dlrs & Drivers for Free Trade | Import Auto Dlrs |
| 8 | $482,695 | Aircraft Owners & Pilots Assn | Air Transport |
| 9 | $475,150 | Americans for Free Intl Trade | Import Auto Dlrs |
| 10 | $453,750 | CSX Corp* | RR/Sea Trans |

* Contributions came from more than one affiliate or subsidiary

# Labor                                                    $43.3 million

*Though many labor unions have found their membership dwindling in recent years, and the political impact of organized labor has been in a long decline — witness their inability to derail the NAFTA agreement — labor unions remain a financial stalwart of the Democratic Party. Union PACs, which account for 99 percent of the labor contributions, delivered $40.6 million to Democratic candidates in the 1992 elections. Republicans got just $2.5 million.*

|  | Total | From PACs | To Dems | To Repubs |
|---|---|---|---|---|
| Building Trade Unions | $6,904,679 | 99% | 94% | 6% |
| Industrial Unions | $10,505,946 | 100% | 98% | 2% |
| Transportation Unions | $10,220,734 | 100% | 91% | 9% |
| Government Worker Unions | $4,449,066 | 100% | 91% | 9% |
| Teacher Unions | $3,477,117 | 100% | 96% | 3% |
| Postal Service Unions | $3,822,198 | 100% | 89% | 10% |
| Other Unions | $3,919,857 | 99% | 97% | 2% |
| TOTAL | $43,299,597 | 99% | 94% | 6% |

## Top 10 Labor Contributors

| Rank | Total | Contributor | Category |
|---|---|---|---|
| 1 | $2,532,956 | Teamsters Union* | Transport Unions |
| 2 | $2,360,017 | National Education Assn* | Teachers |
| 3 | $2,251,489 | United Auto Workers* | Manuf Unions |
| 4 | $1,954,063 | Amer Fedn St/Cnty/Munic Employ* | Govt Unions |
| 5 | $1,661,880 | National Assn of Letter Carriers* | Postal Workers |
| 6 | $1,641,746 | Machinists/Aerospace Workers* | Indust Unions |
| 7 | $1,605,574 | Marine Engineers Union* | Transport Unions |
| 8 | $1,575,999 | IBEW* | Electrical Workers |
| 9 | $1,493,572 | Carpenters & Joiners Union* | Bldg Trades |
| 10 | $1,488,961 | Food & Commercial Workers | Misc Unions |

* Contributions came from more than one affiliate or subsidiary

## Ideological/Single-Issue      $29.3 million

While the most highly-publicized ideological groups are the National Rifle Association and abortion groups, the biggest source of campaign funds among ideological and single-issue groups continues to be the large nationwide network of pro-Israel PACs. The biggest growth in 1992, however, came from women's groups — led by Emily's List, which specializes in bundling large sums to promising Democratic women candidates. Though the Center was able to track more than $3.7 million from women's issue PACs and individual contributors, the real number is undoubtedly much higher, since only contributions of $200 and above are itemized under federal law and many of the women's group donations were for smaller amounts.

|  | Total | From PACs | To Dems | To Repubs |
|---|---|---|---|---|
| Republican/Conservative | $2,479,934 | 32% | 2% | 97% |
| Democratic/Liberal | $2,658,027 | 52% | 98% | 1% |
| Leadership PACs | $2,440,935 | 99% | 59% | 41% |
| Foreign & Defense Policy | $918,162 | 67% | 66% | 30% |
| Pro-Israel | $7,401,113 | 54% | 71% | 29% |
| Abortion Policy | $1,804,175 | 71% | 64% | 35% |
| Gun Policy | $2,024,067 | 98% | 39% | 61% |
| Women's Issues | $3,725,735 | 42% | 84% | 9% |
| Human Rights | $2,335,435 | 70% | 86% | 13% |
| Other Issues | $3,544,331 | 83% | 76% | 23% |
| TOTAL | $29,331,914 | 64% | 67% | 31% |

### Top 10 Ideological/Single-Issue Contributors

| Rank | Total | Contributor | Category |
|---|---|---|---|
| 1 | $1,736,446 | National Rifle Assn | Pro-Guns |
| 2 | $999,755 | Emily's List | Women's Issues |
| 3 | $941,650 | Natl Cmte to Preserve Social Security | Sr Citizens |
| 4 | $718,590 | Human Rights Campaign Fund | Gay/Lesbian |
| 5 | $684,000 | National PAC | Pro-Israel |
| 6 | $651,250 | Natl Cmte for an Effective Congress | Dem/Liberal |
| 7 | $612,130 | Sierra Club | Environment |
| 8 | $517,705 | Natl Abortion Rights Action League* | Pro-Choice |
| 9 | $513,067 | Women's Campaign Fund | Women's Issues |
| 10 | $443,062 | League of Conservation Voters* | Environment |

* Contributions came from more than one affiliate or subsidiary

# 2

# THE CAST OF CHARACTERS

**T**he primary funders of political campaigns — the ones who provide the bulk of the campaign dollars year after year — can be broken down not only by industry but by type. Political action committees, or PACs, are the most well known (and the easiest to track), and PACs have long borne the brunt of reformers' outcries that special interests wield too big a role in the funding of campaigns. But PACs are not by any means the only source of campaign cash — as any candidate who has spent countless hours working their never-ending phone lists of potential contributors can testify. Individual contributors are the biggest source of funds for U.S. Senate candidates, and virtually the only source for presidential contenders.* Individual donations are most potent when they are "bundled," or raised *en masse* from executives of a particular company or in an orchestrated campaign by ideological interest groups. But even when they're not bundled, individuals who can be relied on for contributions of $250, $500, $1000 or more have be-

---

* Federal law allows presidential candidates to solicit campaign funds only until the parties' nominating conventions. After that point, private contributions are banned and public money from the income tax check-off is given to each campaign. (What really happens after the conventions is that fundraising shifts to "soft money" which the parties collect to help boost their slate of candidates.)

come a key source of campaign funds for virtually every candidate running for office.

The exact mix of donor types is influenced in great measure by the laws that govern contributions — particularly contribution limits. At the federal level, the limit for PACs is five times the amount that individuals can give ($5,000 per election for PACs versus $1,000 for individuals). That makes the solicitation of PAC funds one of the top priorities for congressional candidates. Many states also set higher contribution limits for PACs, and in those states the same pattern of PAC preference is likely to be found. In states where PACs have the same limits as individuals, however, a different pattern often emerges — particularly if direct corporate contributions are also allowed. In such cases, there's no real advantage to giving through a PAC. More money can be delivered more easily (and less obviously) if the money comes from executives, or from the corporation itself. Whatever the laws in your state, the following rundown of the cast of characters in campaign financing should be useful as you begin tracking the campaign dollars.

## POLITICAL ACTION COMMITTEES

Political action committees are groups of individuals with common interests who want to advance a specific political agenda by contributing financially to candidates who share their views. Their common interest may be ideological, as among the members of the National Rifle Association or the Sierra Club. It may be business-related, in that all the PAC's donors work for the same company, or belong to the same national trade or professional association, like the National Association of Realtors or the American Medical Association. The connection may also be through membership in a labor union. In total dollars, at least at the federal level (and likely at the state level as well), business PACs dominate all others.

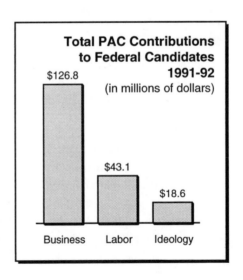

In the 1992 elections, PACs that represent corporations, trade associations and professional groups (such as doctors and lawyers) gave $126.8 million in contributions to federal candidates. (Nearly all of it went to congressional candidates). Labor PACs gave $43.1 million. Ideological and single-issue PACs gave $18.6 million. Together, PACs accounted for about 41 percent of all contributions that went to winning U.S. House candidates, and about 23 percent of the money going to winning Senate candidates.

The reason PACs exist at all is that corporations and labor unions are specifically prohibited from contributing directly to federal candidates. Corporate contributions have been outlawed since 1907. The ban was extended to labor unions in 1943, amid fears in Congress that union walkouts could disrupt the nation's war effort. Organized labor responded to the ban by devising an ingenious workaround. Instead of giving the funds from the union treasury, as they had in the past, unions would collect money from their members, form a "political action committee," and have the PAC give it to candidates on behalf of the union's members. The result was effectively the same, but since the money came from individual union members it was legal — or at least it was not illegal.

The first PAC was formed in 1943 by the Congress of Industrial Organization (which later merged with the American Federation of Labor to form the AFL-CIO). Over the next 30 years, the idea gradually caught on as other unions, then corporations and business groups, formed PACs of their own. But many groups held back. PACs were still a loophole in federal election laws — tolerated, but not officially sanctioned.

In 1974, amid the post-Watergate climate of political reform, Congress gave PACs the green light. In its 1974 amendments to the Federal Election Campaign Act, Congress specifically sanctioned the formation of "political committees" to enable employees of corporations, members of labor unions, or members of professional groups, trade associations or any other political group to pool their dollars and give to the candidates of their choice. At the same time, Congress gave PACs contribution limits that were five times higher than the limits for individuals. It also set up the Federal Election Commission (FEC) to oversee elections and to collect and monitor campaign finance reports filed by PACs, parties and candidates.

The floodgates were now open, and PACs began to proliferate like mushrooms after a spring rain. By the end of 1974, 608 political action committees were officially recognized by the FEC. By mid-1994 that number had grown to just under 4,000. The dollars they pumped into federal elections mushroomed from $12.5 million in 1976 to more than $188 million in the 1991-92 election cycle.


## HOW PACS OPERATE

PACs are as diverse in their structures and agendas as the politicians they give their money to, but there are some broad consistencies in the way most PACs operate. Though these descriptions are based on contributions by federal PACs to congressional candidates, the patterns in most cases are similar to PACs giving in state-level races as well.

• **Most of their money goes to incumbents.** This is particularly true of corporate and other business PACs, which often give more than 90 percent of their contributions to current office-holders. Labor PACs give less — about two-thirds of their dollars went to incumbents in the 1992 elections. Ideological and single-issue PACs are the most likely to give to non-incumbents, though in 1992 even they gave slightly more than half their overall dollars to incumbents. There are several reasons for this strong preference toward incumbents. Since PACs are formed specifically to support candidates, the return on their investment is zero if the candidates they give to lose at the polls. Incumbents, whatever the current political climate, still win far more elections than they lose. That makes them the safest bet for political contributions. Incumbents are also favored because they already hold positions of power. PAC contributions may theoretically be given to help *elect* friendly candidates, but when those candidates face little challenge at the polls, the money is really a way of maintaining an ongoing friendship with politicians in positions of influence. In those cases, it's more a lobbying tool than an election campaign tool.

• **Business PACs tend to be pragmatic, rather than partisan.** Even if most businesses tend to be Republican in their political philosophy, their campaign dollars generally go to whichever politicians hold political power over their interests. At the federal level, Democrats have dominated Congress for nearly 40 years. Not coincidentally, Democrats get the lion's share of PAC contributions, even from industries — like defense and finance — that are hardly thought of as Democratic-leaning. Business PACs are also much more likely to split their money fairly evenly to candidates of both parties, in contrast to labor and ideological PACs, which tend to heavily favor one party or the other.

• **Labor PACs give overwhelmingly to Democrats.** In the 1992 elections, labor PACs at the federal level gave 94 percent of their campaign dollars to Democrats. Labor has always supported Democrats overwhelmingly, but an interesting phenomenon in recent years has been the growing reliance of Democratic incumbents not on their traditional labor support, but on contributions from business groups. The chart on the facing page shows this clearly, comparing business, labor and ideological PAC funds received by freshman Democrats in the U.S. House of Representatives, versus Democrats who were already in office.

• **Many PACs target their biggest gifts to members of key committees** that oversee their interests. (That's not unique to PACs, but it's more common among them.) This is particularly true of businesses whose operations are regulated by government, such as telephone utilities or banks, or those whose business relies on government expenditures or subsidies, like defense contractors or farmers. It's also true of ideological groups. Pro-Israel PACs, for instance, give

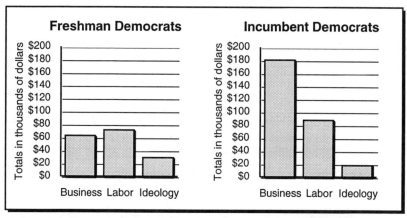

**Shifting loyalties.** This chart shows the dramatic contrast in PAC funding by Democrats in the U.S. House of Representatives in the 1992 elections. On average, newly-elected Democrats relied more on contributions from labor PACs than from business or ideological PACs. Incumbent Democrats, on the other hand, got about twice as much on average from business PACs as from organized labor, with ideological PACs supplying negligible support. The chart helps explain the erosion in labor's success on Capitol Hill, even among their traditional Democratic allies.

heavily to members of the Foreign Affairs and Foreign Relations committees in Congress.

• **PACs tend to be consistent givers.** Contribution levels do tend to peak when important legislation is about to be considered, but most PACs are fairly consistent in their giving from year to year. Most political action committees, and most big contributors in general, are involved in the political system over the long haul. Only rarely does a PAC emerge out of nowhere, give a lot of money when its issue comes before Congress, then disappear when their bill is passed. Most PACs represent organizations that have issues before Congress year after year. Their contribution patterns reflect that continuing interest, and are generally designed to build solid, long-term relationships with members of Congress.

One final word that's important to keep in mind: PACs are a major source of campaign funds, but they're by no means the only source. Large individual contributions account for at least as much in federal races, particularly in races for the U.S. Senate. In presidential races, PAC contributions typically make up only a minuscule percentage of the total dollars raised.

Also important: at the federal level, certain industries give more money through individual contributions than through PACs. The most important of these are lawyers and lobbyists. In 1992, nearly 86 percent of the money they gave came through individual contributions, not through PACs. About half the money from doctors and other health professionals came from individual donations. Three-quarters of the contribution dollars from the securities and real estate industries came from individual donors. If you're trying to get a sense of which industries are giving how much, you need to go beyond the PACs when you're looking at those industries. On the other hand, nearly 100 percent of labor contributions on the federal level are made through PACs.

Because of this, studies that examine only PAC contributions are virtually certain to be overcounting labor contributions and greatly undercounting the money coming from lawyers and lobbyists, real estate agents, the securities industry, and several others. Here's a list of the industries that gave most heavily through individual contributions in the 1992 federal elections:

| Industries with Lowest Pct from PACs | | |
|---|---|---|
| Industry/Interest | Total 91-92 | PAC Pct |
| Non-Profit Institutions | $870,993 | 0% |
| Retired | $15,930,210 | 0% |
| Education | $4,341,833 | 3% |
| Recreation/Live Entertainment | $471,492 | 4% |
| Lobbyists/PR | $5,821,253 | 4% |
| Business Services | $7,502,660 | 10% |
| Printing & Publishing | $3,059,581 | 15% |
| Lawyers/Law Firms | $38,237,491 | 16% |
| Miscellaneous Services | $1,564,313 | 19% |
| Building Materials & Equipment | $2,869,672 | 23% |
| Securities & Investment | $15,936,222 | 23% |
| Real Estate | $16,472,555 | 23% |
| Special Trade Contractors | $1,686,428 | 24% |
| Lodging/Tourism | $1,595,139 | 25% |

Whatever the financial clout of PACs in your state, they do remain an important starting point for any analysis of money in politics. Because the number of PACs is limited, and their interests are generally easy to pinpoint, PACs are the quickest and easiest block of campaign funds to identify. If you haven't got the time or resources to track individual dollars and classify them by industry and interest group, at least track the PACs. They don't represent all the money by any means, but they're certainly major players in modern American politics.

## CONTRIBUTIONS FROM INDIVIDUALS

Generally speaking, the more expensive the race, the more important the role of large contributions from individual givers. Many campaigns tout the fact that most of their contributions come in small denominations from "regular folks." In total numbers of contributors, that's usually correct. But in total *dollars*, most big-budget campaigns rely far more heavily on big donors than on small ones. In the 1992 congressional races, for example, the average U.S. House member collected just 19 percent of their total dollars from individuals giving under $200. Only 10 of the 435 members collected more than half their dollars from small donors.

Spaghetti feeds and hot dogs in the park may be popular ways of involving the voters and raising a little cash, but most candidates spend far more time working their telephone lists of potential donors who can give $250, $500, $1000 or more. One of the biggest problems they face, in fact, is that federal campaign laws, as well as most states, set limits on how much individuals can give. Wealthy contributors who want to give more routinely add donations from their spouses or other family members to bolster their giving. At both the federal and state level, contributions from "homemakers" and "housewives" are profuse. Contributions from children — usually identified as "students" on federal reports — also appear, though not nearly as often.

In low-spending campaigns, and occasionally in high-spending campaigns as well, a majority of campaign funds may come from small donations under the amount that needs to be itemized on campaign spending reports. If the campaign is a big-spending one, a high proportion of small contributions is a sign of one of two things — either it's a genuine grass-roots campaign or the candidate is drawing most of his or her funds through direct mail solicitations. If it's a direct mail operation, you'll almost always find unusually high expenditures for mail.

One interesting note: campaigns that do draw a large proportion of small contributions (without relying on heavy direct mail appeals) usually do very well at the polls. Non-incumbent candidates who rely primarily on money from their own pocket, or a combination of their own money plus a high proportion of large individual donations, often lose at the polls to candidates who spend less, but rely more heavily on small donations.

## LAWYERS & LOBBYISTS

A special case in individual contributions are those that come from lawyers, lobbyists and other political "rainmakers" whose contributions are often given not only on their own behalf, but indirectly on behalf of their clients. Lobbyists in particular are among the most active contributors in the political world. They are the ultimate political operatives, and they know probably better than anyone how important campaign dollars are to politicians. Furthermore, the financial influence of lobbyists often extends far beyond their own contributions. Lobbyists quite often advise their clients on where and how to spread their contributions. Lobbyists may also help arrange fundraisers for lawmakers, and even sit on their fundraising committees.

One thing to be aware of: the number of *de facto* lobbyists is often much higher than the number of officially registered lobbyists. In Washington, D.C., for example, only a small proportion of lawyers and lobbyists who do lobbying work on behalf of clients are actually registered as lobbyists. Lobby reform legislation may change that situation; time will tell.

The patterns by which lobbyists (and some lawyers) give their money often resembles the patterns seen with PACs — that is, rather than giving a lot of money to a few candidates, lobbyists tend to give relatively small amounts — $250 or so — to many different candidates, nearly all of whom are incumbents. Access to lawmakers is the name of the game for lobbyists. Their contributions help get them in the door, and help cement a friendly, long-term relationship.

## PARTY CONTRIBUTIONS

At the federal level, party contributions are usually a fairly small proportion of a candidate's overall funding. However, in addition to direct contributions to candidates, additional "coordinated expenditures" may also be made by the parties. These funds, spent by the party in concert with the candidates' campaign, can amount to considerably more, particularly in Senate races.

At the state level, party contributions — whether from the state party or from local jurisdictions — can be very important sources of campaign cash. If that's the case in your state, be wary of "pass-through" contributions which go to party committees and then are passed along to specific candidates. Such contributions are an easy way to bypass contribution limits, essentially using the party committees to launder the money and obscure its real source.

Such pass-through contributions are one reason why it's important to keep tabs not just on candidate contribution reports, but also on those filed by the national, state and local party committees.

## CANDIDATE CONTRIBUTIONS

Wealthy candidates have a big advantage over those with more modest personal resources — they don't have to rely on outside donors to jump start their campaigns. The U.S. Supreme Court has ruled (in *Buckley v. Valeo*) that no limits can be set on what an individual can contribute to his or her own campaign, so a wealthy individual can spend as much as he or she wants (witness Ross Perot).

A number of millionaire candidates have tried to turn this to their advantage. When Wisconsin businessman Herb Kohl financed his campaign for the U.S. Senate in 1988 with $7 million of his own money, his slogan was "He's nobody's man but yours." Kohl won in a close election. In 1992, Republican Michael Huffington vastly eclipsed the previous record for spending in a U.S.

House race, putting $5.2 million of his own money into his successful campaign in California. Huffington was back in 1994, aiming to unseat California Senator Dianne Feinstein with an even bigger bundle of funds from his personal fortune.

While early money in any election can be crucial to drawing other outside funds later, the willingness of candidates to spend large sums of their own money doesn't necessarily mean they will turn down contributions later. In fact, candidates who win public office often repay themselves for the "loans" they made to their campaign, sometimes years after the election. This should set off alarm bells for any reporter tracking the money, since such contributions go directly into the candidate's pocket.

## CORPORATIONS AND OTHER BUSINESSES

As of mid-1994, 29 states allowed direct contributions by corporations and other businesses to candidates for state legislative and other offices. Such contributions are illegal in federal elections, and have been since the passage of the Tillman Act in 1907. As a means around this prohibition, many corporations, trade associations, professional groups and other businesses sponsor political action committees that collect funds from their employees or members and funnel them to candidates. Such PAC contributions are legal in all states, and at the federal level.

## LABOR UNIONS

Like corporations, labor unions are prohibited from contributing directly to federal candidates. Some 39 states do allow direct union contributions to state-level candidates, however. Unions may also give through political action committees, whose funds are collected from union members.

Unions traditionally are the staunchest organized supporters of the Democratic Party. Some of that support shows up in campaign finance reports, but much of it — particularly volunteer work in phone banks and other campaign efforts — does not.

## IDEOLOGICAL & SINGLE-ISSUE GROUPS

Although most of the money in federal elections comes from business or labor groups, some of the most high-profile campaign contributors are groups affiliated around ideological or single-issue platforms. Abortion rights — both pro and con — is one issue that draws not only controversy, but plenty of money as well. Gun control is another hot-button issue. Less visible, but considerably better financed, is the nationwide collection of groups that support closer U.S. ties to Israel. The fastest-growing ideological segment in the 1992 elections were groups aiming to elect more women candidates.

To translate their political will into practical help for candidates, ideological and single-issue groups tend to form their own PACs, whether national, local, or both. A number of groups go beyond PAC contributions, however, and actively "bundle" individual contributions to candidates as well. Emily's List, a national PAC that supports the election of Democratic women to Congress, claimed to have delivered $6 million to women candidates in the 1992 elections. The Center was able to document just under $1 million of that, though much of the money was undoubtedly delivered in small contributions that are not itemized at the federal level.

# 3

## LOOPHOLES

**B**ehind every campaign finance law — and particularly every contribution limit — there lurks a loophole waiting to emerge. Wealthy contributors with money to give and reasons to give it have proven particularly artful in navigating through the nuances of the laws in ways that have enabled the contribution limits to be stretched, suspended, or totally cast aside.

Some loopholes have become institutionalized. Political action committees were loopholes when they were first invented in the 1940s. They have since become fully sanctioned in federal law and in the laws of all 50 states. Other loopholes have become so commonplace they've become accepted by default. If you're a wealthy executive and you want to double the amount you can deliver to a particular candidate, for example, all you need do is enlist your spouse to give a contribution of his or her own. If you've got children, they too can give in most states — and the more you have, the bigger your family's potential contribution.

But many other loopholes still exist, and through them are delivered millions of dollars every election year. Here's a quick guide to three of the most important — bundling, independent expenditures and soft money.

## BUNDLING

Besides giving through family members, major donors may also "bundle" the contributions of many individuals and present them to the candidate in a block. Technically, bundling refers to the practice of collecting checks from a number of individuals, putting them together in a bundle, and handing them over to the candidate *en masse*. The candidate understands that the bundle came not from isolated individuals, but from the group — as in a dozen executives (plus their spouses) from a single company. Often the money is collected at a specific fundraising event hosted by the company that's giving. Other times, the money will flow in over a period of days or even weeks. In either case, the donors and the recipient both understand that these are not isolated contributions, but a block of gifts coming from the same source.

Identifying the affiliations of the contributors is crucial to uncovering these operations, since bundling is the most efficient way (and the most common way) for one group to deliver large contributions to a single candidate, while still staying within the laws on contribution limits.

Bundling per se is not illegal. What *is* illegal, however, at the federal level and in the states, is reimbursement by the contributors' employer. If a dozen members of a New York law firm, for example, hold a fundraiser for a U.S. Senate candidate and each give $1,000, that's fine. If the firm then awards $1,000 "bonuses" to the contributors to repay them, that's illegal.

Such contributions would be, in effect, corporate contributions, which are outlawed under federal law. Even in states where corporate contributions are legal, reimbursed contributions may still run afoul of the law. Since the money was really coming from a corporation, and not an individual, such gifts could be considered "contributions in the name of another" which are generally illegal. Check with elections officials in your state if you come across such a case.


## INDEPENDENT EXPENDITURES

Under federal election laws, strict limits apply to contributions that can go directly to candidates, but no such limits apply if an organization runs an independent campaign — even if the campaign supports or attacks a specific candidate. The only caveat is that the independent campaign must not be coordinated in any way with the campaign of any candidate.

The biggest and most visible independent expenditure campaigns tend to occur in presidential election years — the famous "Willie Horton" ads that attacked Michael Dukakis in 1988 were a notable example. But in every election, a handful of congressional candidates also benefit (or suffer) from independent campaigns. In 1992, six groups ran independent expenditure campaigns amounting to half a million dollars or more, as seen in the following table:

## Top PACs Making Independent Expenditures in 1992

| Contributor | Total | Target Races |
|---|---|---|
| Presidential Victory Committee | $2,057,757 | Presidential |
| National Right to Life PAC | $1,614,440 | Pres/House/Senate |
| American Medical Assn | $1,024,210 | House/Senate |
| National Assn of Realtors | $999,016 | House/Senate |
| National Rifle Assn | $957,666 | House/Senate |
| National Abortion Rights Action League | $718,756 | House/Senate |

### "SOFT MONEY"

In the eyes of many observers — and many political practitioners who make use of it — the principal loophole in the federal campaign spending law is something that has come to be called "soft money." In the broadest sense, soft money encompasses any contributions not regulated by federal election laws. The exemption was made to encourage "party-building" activities that benefit the political parties in general, but not specific candidates. In reality, though, the loophole has emerged as the parties' primary means of raising tens of millions of dollars in unlimited amounts from wealthy contributors during the fall presidential campaigns, when direct contributions to candidates are prohibited. They are also used to support congressional candidates in key battleground states during off-year elections.

Technically, soft money contributions are supposed to be used only for state and local political activities — such as voter registration, get-out-the-vote drives and bumper stickers — and for such generic party-building activities as TV ads supporting the Democratic and Republican platforms, but not naming specific candidates. Typically, however, the funds pay for much more — including office overhead, the purchase of expensive computer equipment and other behind-the-scenes expenses — thus freeing up other contributions to the party to be used to directly support candidates.

During the 1992 presidential campaign, the Democratic and Republican parties raised an estimated $34 million and $48 million respectively in soft money contributions on the national level alone. The exact figures will never be known (except to the parties), however, because much of the soft money was contributed directly to state and local political committees.

Soft money is such a popular fundraising tool for the parties for four main reasons:

• **Soft money is not subject to any contribution limits at all.** The biggest soft money donor in the 1992 elections was the Archer-Daniels-Midland Co. and its top corporate officers. They gave a combined total of nearly $1.4 million — most of it to the Republican Party. That's 140 times the limit that could be given by the company's PAC, if the contributions were made to a candidate.

• Soft money can be given by anyone — including groups prohibited from making contributions to federal candidates or parties. Corporations and labor unions, which are banned from contributing directly to candidates or to the parties, can (and do) dip directly into their corporate or union treasuries for soft money contributions.

• Soft money offers an extra means of political giving for individuals who've already given the maximum to candidates and federal parties. Under the federal election laws, individual contributors are limited to an annual maximum of $25,000 in contributions to all candidates, PACs and national parties. Once they've "maxed out" they can give no more — except in soft money, where all limits are off.

• Soft money offers a way for corporations, unions and wealthy contributors to directly support presidential candidates in the fall elections. Since 1974, when Congress authorized the $1 checkoff on federal income tax returns (since raised to $3), presidential elections have been publicly financed. Once the primaries are over, and the parties have officially nominated their candidates at their summer conventions, no more private contributions are allowed. Because of the soft money loophole, however, the period during the fall campaign has turned into the most intensive period of fundraising in American politics. In 1988 the Republicans even organized an exclusive club — called "Team 100" — made up of soft money contributors who gave $100,000 or more. In 1992, Team 100 was back, giving more than ever. Not to be outdone, the Democrats created a new circle of elite givers called the "Managing Trustees." Admission to this blue-chip group requires giving or raising at least $200,000 in soft money. Both the Bush and Clinton administrations rewarded a number of their top soft money contributors with ambassadorships and other political favors.

The list on the opposite page highlights the 20 biggest soft money contributors to the national parties in the 1991-92 election cycle.

## Top Soft Money Contributors in 1991-92

| Rank | Contributor | Total | To Repubs | To Dems |
|------|-------------|-------|-----------|---------|
| 1 | Archer-Daniels-Midland* | $1,374,500 | $1,107,000 | $267,500 |
| 2 | RJR Nabisco* | $875,305 | $529,305 | $346,000 |
| 3 | Atlantic Richfield Co* | $857,958 | $579,641 | $278,317 |
| 4 | Philip Morris* | $816,580 | $589,080 | $227,500 |
| 5 | Joseph E Seagram & Sons | $731,637 | $524,727 | $206,910 |
| 6 | American Financial Corp | $715,000 | $715,000 | $0 |
| 7 | US Tobacco | $652,768 | $525,004 | $127,764 |
| 8 | International Marketing Bureau | $633,770 | $633,770 | $0 |
| 9 | Merrill Lynch* | $594,900 | $485,100 | $109,800 |
| 10 | New Jersey Gala '92 | $566,286 | $0 | $566,286 |
| 11 | National Education Assn | $423,752 | $7,750 | $416,002 |
| 12 | United Steelworkers | $404,876 | $0 | $404,876 |
| 13 | Time Warner* | $398,573 | $100,240 | $298,333 |
| 14 | Chevron Corp | $361,760 | $256,372 | $105,388 |
| 15 | Occidental Petroleum | $336,030 | $224,080 | $111,950 |
| 16 | Sony Corp of America | $332,650 | $100,000 | $232,650 |
| 17 | American Intertrade Group* | $322,800 | $322,800 | $0 |
| 18 | Tobacco Institute | $317,202 | $164,927 | $152,275 |
| 19 | Alida Rockefeller Messinger | $300,650 | $0 | $300,650 |
| 20 | Goldman, Sachs & Co | $293,520 | $248,520 | $45,000 |

* Total came from more than one affiliate or subsidiary.

The above list includes contributions made to the Democratic and National Committees, as well as the National Republican Senatorial Committee, the Democratic Senatorial Campaign Committee, the National Republican Congressional Committee, the Democratic Congressional Campaign Committee, the President's Dinner Committee and the Democratic Congressional Dinner Committee.

Tens of millions of *additional* soft money dollars — often given by the same contributors — also flow directly to state parties every election year. In the 1992 elections, the Center investigated records in nine states — Colorado, Florida, Illinois, Iowa, Missouri, Ohio, Oregon, Pennsylvania and Texas — and uncovered nearly $37 million in soft money contributions to state party committees.

# 4

# THE INCUMBENT'S EDGE

One of the first patterns apparent when you start examining campaign records is the huge disparity between two very different classes of candidates — those who are already incumbents and those who are on the outside trying to get in.

The industry spending patterns seen in the previous pages, by and large, apply mainly to *incumbent* members of Congress. That's where the overwhelming majority of congressional campaign dollars are directed. Although PACs can and do represent groups from every segment of the political spectrum, most tend to be conservative in one respect: they want to put their money with candidates who have a much better-than-average chance of actually winning election. The easiest way to insure that their money will go to someone who will likely win is to put it with politicians who are already in office. And by and large, incumbents do win.

Congressional reelection rates have long been stratospheric, at least in the House of Representatives. Even in the "throw-the-bums out" elections of 1992, those seeking reelection still managed to win 88 percent of the time — and that was the lowest reelection rate since 1974. From 1984 to 1990, the

House reelection rate never dipped below 95 percent. Senators seeking new terms are also good bets, though not as solid as House members. In the Reagan landslide of 1980, nine Senate Democrats lost at the polls, dropping the reelection rate that year to 55 percent. Since 1982, the rate has never dipped below 75 percent; it was 83 percent in 1992.

Well aware of such statistics, federal PACs sponsored by corporations, trade associations and other business groups are particularly loathe to spend their dollars on non-incumbents. Many business PACs spend 90 percent or more of their campaign dollars supporting incumbents, with only token amounts going to challengers and open seat candidates.

Labor PACs are somewhat less restrictive. Besides giving heavily to incumbent Democrats (and sparingly to a few Republicans), they generally direct funds to the most promising Democratic challengers, or those in open-seat races thought to have a good chance of winning. Even so, labor PACs as a whole still give nearly two-thirds of their contributions to incumbents.

The one sector of PACs that does tend to be somewhat more open to non-incumbents are the ideological and single-issue groups. But even these PACs still give a slight majority of their overall dollars to incumbents.

Since most of those big-donor dollars from established interest groups are going to incumbents, virtually every incumbent has a base of support that is simply not available to those not already in office. The funding disparity can be seen most glaringly at the congressional level, when comparing average campaign spending of incumbents versus those of challengers. The figures point to a huge, and still growing, spending gap, as seen in the chart below.

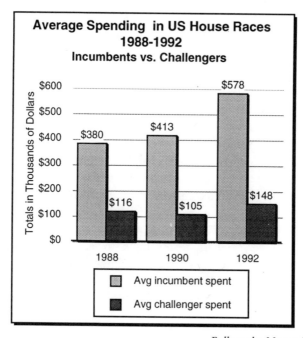

Another statistic that underlines the massive inequality between funding of congressional candidates: in each of the past three election cycles (1988, 1990 and 1992) in more than half the congressional districts in the nation the winning candidate spent at least *ten times* the amount spent by the loser. (The figure includes incumbents running unopposed.) In nearly every case, the winner was an incumbent.

Candidates who have more money don't always win, but they win far more than they lose. More important, the odds against those who are severely underfunded are daunting indeed. In the 1992 congressional elections — an unusually open year for Congress since the record crop of retirements produced a large number of open seat races — the odds of a challenger's winning were directly proportional to the amount they spent. The chart below tells the tale:

| Amount Spent by Challenger | Odds of Winning |
| --- | --- |
| $0 or unreported | 0 |
| $1-$99,999 | 0 |
| $100,000-$249,999 | 13:1 |
| $250,000-$499,999 | 4:1 |
| $500,000 & over | 2:1 |

Though this charts spotlights congressional races, the same trend — if not the same set of odds — could likely be seen at every level of public office around the country. Except in local races where spending levels are low for all candidates, the amount of available money is often the strongest single determinant of who wins and who loses on election day.

## COMMITTEE ASSIGNMENTS INFLUENCE GIVING

Once a candidate has won election and joined the ranks of political incumbents, the patterns in their campaign contributions undergo an important and often dramatic shift. A typical member of Congress, for instance, collects the bulk of their campaign funds not only from constituents in their home district, but also from a new set of "cash constituents" whose interests are more directly tied to the member's committee assignments on Capitol Hill.

PAC contributions in particular tend to follow committee assignments, if members sit on committees of importance to specific industries or interest. Agriculture committee members, for example, tower over all other members of Congress in receipt of funds from agribusiness. Banks give most heavily to members of the banking committees. Defense contractors give the biggest share of their dollars to members on the Armed Services and Appropriations committees. Further, when a member of Congress changes committees, their profile of leading contributors changes too.

Individual contributions, in general, are more reflective of the home district's economy. Texans, for example, get plenty of oil money, Midwesterners tend to get a lot from farmers, and so on. The one exception to this general rule is when a high proportion of the member's money comes from out-of-state — particularly when it comes from the Washington, D.C. area. That money tends to come heavily from lobbyists, and from committee-related donors.

Many committees of Congress don't have jurisdiction over a particular industry — the Rules Committee or Veterans Affairs Committee, for example. Others, like the tax-writing Ways and Means Committee, have interests important to *every* sector of the business community. Industry patterns are not as strongly defined in those committees as they are in more industry-specific committees.

As you can see in the industry profiles on pages 5-16, most industries split their money relatively evenly between Democrats and Republicans. But one big difference between the two parties is in their contributions from organized labor. Labor gives the overwhelming majority of its dollars to Democrats — 94 percent in the 1992 elections. So Democratic members typically get a major portion of their dollars from labor PACs. Republicans (unless they sit on committees of particular importance to labor) generally get very little labor money.

One other important point that deserves note: few members of Congress get a majority of their campaign dollars from any single industry. There are simply so many different interest groups with a stake in legislation that nearly all members get at least a little bit from everybody. Typically, one sector will give more than the others, and this most often relates to the member's committee assignment. But it's simply not the case (or only rarely the case) that one member of Congress gets, say, 70 or 80 percent or more of their money from a single industry or interest. (The one exception to that general rule is that some liberal Democrats get so little support from business groups that their contributions from organized labor account for the bulk of their campaign dollars.)

# 5

# RULES OF THE GAME

**C**ampaign finance laws vary widely from state to state, and even within states from jurisdiction to jurisdiction. Another set of laws applies to races for Congress and the presidency. One rule, however, is consistent at all levels of political office: foreign nationals who do not have permanent residence in the United States are prohibited from contributing to any political candidates in the U.S. — at the federal, state, or local level.

That federal law does not apply, however, to political action committees operated by U.S. subsidiaries of foreign companies, as long as the members of the PAC are U.S. citizens. Sony Corp. of America, for example, can — and does — sponsor a PAC that contributes to federal candidates. Many other foreign-held companies also contribute through their employee PACs.

Aside from banning non-resident aliens from contributing, the nation's campaign finance laws are a patchwork quilt. Contribution limits in different states vary from $500 in Florida and Kentucky to unlimited sums, at least for some contributors, in 23 states. All states, and the federal government, require disclosure of contributions to candidates, but the threshold for itemizing contributions varies widely, as does the information required to be disclosed.

Nearly all states require the name and addresses of the contributors to be listed,* and all require the date and amount of the contribution to be disclosed. Many states, and the federal government, also require contributors to disclose their occupation and employer. For reporters trying to find the patterns in the contributions, the inclusion of occupation/employer information is the single most important element of disclosure. If the donors' employers or occupations are not listed, you'll have to dig out that information through other means, and the job of identifying the economic interests behind candidates and elected officials will be much more difficult.

Keep in mind that campaign finance laws, like all laws, are revised from time to time. The U.S. House and Senate each passed their own versions of campaign reform legislation in 1994, but differences between the two bills were never resolved and the legislation died in the closing days of the 103rd Congress. State and local governments also revise their laws from time to time. Check with the state you're interested in for the latest information — the phone numbers are listed on pages 59-69. Another important note: this book concentrates only on contributions to candidates. Different limits apply to contributions to political parties and to PACs. Contact the relevant agencies for information on those limits.

The list on the following pages shows current contribution limits and disclosure requirements at the federal and state levels. For more detailed information on limits, disclosure requirements, availability of records and nuances of local laws, contact the specific agencies directly.

NOTE: Many states tie their contribution limits not to the calendar year or the full two-year election cycle, but to specific elections. *In those cases, primaries, general elections, special elections and runoffs are each considered separate elections.* In the listings on the following pages, a limit of "$1,000/ election," for example, indicates that a contributor could give $1,000 to a candidate for the primary election and another $1,000 for the general election. If there were a runoff or a special election, they could give even more.

---

* The exceptions are Montana and Wyoming, which require only the donor's name, city and state; and West Virginia, which requires only the donor's name for contributions under $250.

## ALABAMA

*Individuals:* Unlimited
*Corporations:* $500/election
*Unions:* Unlimited
*PACs:* Unlimited

## ALASKA

*Individuals:* $1,000/year
*Corporations:* $1,000/year
*Unions:* $1,000/year
*PACs:* $1,000/year

## ARIZONA

*Individuals:* $640/year for statewide candidates, $250 for others
*Corporations:* Prohibited
*Unions:* Prohibited
*PACs:* $3,200/year for statewide candidates, $1,270 for others

## ARKANSAS

*Individuals:* $1,000/election
*Corporations:* $1,000/election
*Unions:* $1,000/election
*PACs:* $1,000/election

## CALIFORNIA

*Individuals:* Unlimited except for special elections or special election runoffs, where limit is $1,000/election.

*Corporations:* Unlimited except for special elections or special election runoffs, where limit is $1,000/election.

*Unions:* Same limits as individuals and corporations, unless registered as a PAC, in which case PAC limits apply.

*PACs:* Unlimited except for special elections or special election runoffs, where limit is $5,000/election for "broad based" PACs or $2,500/election for other PACs.

## COLORADO

*Individuals:* Unlimited
*Corporations:* Unlimited
*Unions:* Unlimited
*PACs:* Unlimited

## CONNECTICUT

| | |
|---|---|
| *Individuals:* | $250-$2,500/election depending on office |
| *Corporations:* | Prohibited |
| *Unions:* | Prohibited |
| *PACs:* | Business & labor PACs: $250-$5,000/election depending on office and type of PAC. PACs of two or more individuals (not affiliated with business, labor, trade or professional associations) can give unlimited amounts. |

## DELAWARE

| | |
|---|---|
| *Individuals:* | $1,200 statewide/election, $600 other/election |
| *Corporations:* | $1,200 statewide/election, $600 other/election |
| *Unions:* | $1,200 statewide/election, $600 other/election |
| *PACs:* | $1,200 statewide/election, $600 other/election |

## FLORIDA

| | |
|---|---|
| *Individuals:* | $500/election ($100 for unemancipated children under 18) |
| *Corporations:* | $500/election |
| *Unions:* | $500/election |
| *PACs:* | $500/election |

## GEORGIA

| | |
|---|---|
| *Individuals:* | $2,500 statewide candidates/election, $1,000 others/election |
| *Corporations:* | $2,500 statewide candidates/election, $1,000 others/election |
| *Unions:* | $2,500 statewide candidates/election, $1,000 others/election |
| *PACs:* | $2,500 statewide candidates/election, $1,000 others/election |

## HAWAII

| | |
|---|---|
| *Individuals:* | $2,000/election |
| *Corporations:* | $2,000/election |
| *Unions:* | $2,000/election |
| *PACs:* | $2,000/election |

## IDAHO

| | |
|---|---|
| *Individuals:* | Unlimited |
| *Corporations:* | Unlimited |
| *Unions:* | Unlimited |
| *PACs:* | Unlimited |

## ILLINOIS

| | |
|---|---|
| *Individuals:* | Unlimited |
| *Corporations:* | Unlimited |
| *Unions:* | Unlimited |
| *PACs:* | Unlimited |

## INDIANA

| | |
|---|---|
| *Individuals:* | Unlimited |
| *Corporations:* | $5,000/statewide candidates, $2,000/others |
| *Unions:* | $5,000/statewide candidates, $2,000/others |
| *PACs:* | Unlimited |

## IOWA

| | |
|---|---|
| *Individuals:* | Unlimited |
| *Corporations:* | Prohibited |
| *Unions:* | May only give a total of $250 to all candidates. Otherwise, they must form a PAC. |
| *PACs:* | Unlimited |

## KANSAS

| | |
|---|---|
| *Individuals:* | $500-$2,000/election cycle depending on office |
| *Corporations:* | $500-$2,000/election cycle depending on office |
| *Unions:* | $500-$2,000/election cycle depending on office |
| *PACs:* | $500-$2,000/election cycle depending on office |

## KENTUCKY

| | |
|---|---|
| *Individuals:* | $500/election ($100 for minors) |
| *Corporations:* | Prohibited |
| *Unions:* | $500/election |
| *PACs:* | $500/election |

## LOUISIANA

| | |
|---|---|
| *Individuals:* | $1,000-$5,000/election, depending on office |
| *Corporations:* | $1,000-$5,000/election, depending on office |
| *Unions:* | $1,000-$5,000/election, depending on office |
| *PACs:* | $1,000-$5,000/election, depending on office. Limit is double for large PACs (those with over 200 members who give at least $50/year). |

## MAINE

| | |
|---|---|
| *Individuals:* | $1,000/election |
| *Corporations:* | $5,000/election |
| *Unions:* | $5,000/election |
| *PACs:* | $5,000/election |

## MARYLAND

*Individuals:*    $4,000
*Corporations:*    $4,000
*Unions:*    $4,000
*PACs:*    $6,000/four-year election cycle

## MASSACHUSETTS

*Individuals:*    $1,000/year ($25 for minors). Limit drops to $500 beginning in 1995.
*Corporations:*    Prohibited
*Unions:*    Technically unlimited, unless total contributions exceed $15,000 or 10% of gross revenues. In that case, contributions must be reported and are subject to the same limits as PACs.
*PACs:*    $1,000. Limit drops to $500 beginning in 1995, and candidates will have a ceiling on total PAC contributions they may accept.

## MICHIGAN

*Individuals:*    $500-$3,400 depending on office
*Corporations:*    Prohibited
*Unions:*    $500-$3,400 depending on office
*PACs:*    $500-$3,400 depending on office. PACs that qualify as independent committees may give 10 times that amount.

## MINNESOTA

*Individuals:*    $100-$2,000 depending on office & year
*Corporations:*    Prohibited
*Unions:*    $100-$2,000 depending on office & year, if registered as a PAC
*PACs:*    $100-$2,000 depending on office & year

## MISSISSIPPI

*Individuals:*    Unlimited
*Corporations:*    $1,000/election cycle
*Unions:*    Unlimited
*PACs:*    Unlimited

## MISSOURI

*Individuals:*    Unlimited through 1994. Starting in 1995 limits range from $250-$1,000/election depending on office.
*Corporations:*    Unlimited. Effective Jan. 1, 1995 limits range from $250-$1,000/election depending on office
*Unions:*    Unlimited. Effective Jan. 1, 1995 limits range from $250-$1,000/election depending on office
*PACs:*    Unlimited. Effective Jan. 1, 1995 limits range from $250-$1,000/election depending on office

### MONTANA

| | |
|---|---|
| *Individuals:* | $250-$1,500 depending on office |
| *Corporations:* | Prohibited |
| *Unions:* | $300-$8,000 depending on office |
| *PACs:* | $300-$8,000 depending on office |

### NEBRASKA

| | |
|---|---|
| *Individuals:* | Unlimited |
| *Corporations:* | Unlimited |
| *Unions:* | Unlimited |
| *PACs:* | Unlimited |

### NEVADA

| | |
|---|---|
| *Individuals:* | $10,000/election cycle for statewide candidates, $2,000/election cycle for others |
| *Corporations:* | $20,000/election cycle for statewide candidates, $10,000/election cycle for others |
| *Unions:* | $20,000/election cycle for statewide candidates, $10,000/election cycle for others |
| *PACs:* | $20,000/election cycle for statewide candidates, $10,000/election cycle for others |

### NEW HAMPSHIRE

| | |
|---|---|
| *Individuals:* | $5,000/election if candidate accepts spending limits, otherwise $1,000/election |
| *Corporations:* | Prohibited |
| *Unions:* | Prohibited |
| *PACs:* | Unlimited if candidate accepts spending limits, otherwise $1,000/election |

### NEW JERSEY

| | |
|---|---|
| *Individuals:* | $1,800/election for governor candidates, $1,500/election for others |
| *Corporations:* | $1,800/election for governor candidates, $1,500/election for others |
| *Unions:* | $1,800/election for governor candidates, $1,500/election for others |
| *PACs:* | $1,800/election for governor candidates, $5,000/election for others |

### NEW MEXICO

| | |
|---|---|
| *Individuals:* | Unlimited |
| *Corporations:* | Unlimited |
| *Unions:* | Unlimited |
| *PACs:* | Unlimited |

## NEW YORK

| | |
|---|---|
| *Individuals:* | $1,000-$25,000 depending on office & election |
| *Corporations:* | $1,000-$5,000/year depending on office & election. Limit of $5,000 to all candidates per year. |
| *Unions:* | $1,000-$25,000 depending on office & election |
| *PACs:* | $1,000-$25,000 depending on office & election |

## NORTH CAROLINA

| | |
|---|---|
| *Individuals:* | $4,000/election |
| *Corporations:* | Prohibited |
| *Unions:* | Prohibited |
| *PACs:* | $4,000/election |

## NORTH DAKOTA

| | |
|---|---|
| *Individuals:* | Unlimited |
| *Corporations:* | Prohibited |
| *Unions:* | Prohibited |
| *PACs:* | Unlimited |

## OHIO

| | |
|---|---|
| *Individuals:* | Unlimited |
| *Corporations:* | Prohibited |
| *Unions:* | Unlimited |
| *PACs:* | Unlimited |

## OKLAHOMA

| | |
|---|---|
| *Individuals:* | $5,000/year |
| *Corporations:* | Prohibited |
| *Unions:* | $5,000/year |
| *PACs:* | $5,000/year |

## OREGON

| | |
|---|---|
| *Individuals:* | Unlimited |
| *Corporations:* | Unlimited |
| *Unions:* | Unlimited |
| *PACs:* | Unlimited |

## PENNSYLVANIA

| | |
|---|---|
| *Individuals:* | Unlimited |
| *Corporations:* | Prohibited |
| *Unions:* | Prohibited |
| *PACs:* | Unlimited |

### RHODE ISLAND

*Individuals:* $1,000/year. $2,000/year if candidate qualifies for public funding.
*Corporations:* Prohibited
*Unions:* Prohibited
*PACs:* $1,000/year

### SOUTH CAROLINA

*Individuals:* $3,500/election cycle for statewide candidates, $1,000/election cycle for others
*Corporations:* $3,500/election cycle for statewide candidates, $1,000/election cycle for others
*Unions:* $3,500/election cycle for statewide candidates, $1,000/election cycle for others
*PACs:* $3,500/election cycle for statewide candidates, $1,000/election cycle for others

### SOUTH DAKOTA

*Individuals:* $1,000/year for statewide candidates, $250/year for others
*Corporations:* Prohibited
*Unions:* Prohibited unless they form a PAC
*PACs:* Unlimited

### TENNESSEE

*Individuals:* Unlimited
*Corporations:* Prohibited
*Unions:* Unlimited, if they register as a PAC
*PACs:* Unlimited

### TEXAS

*Individuals:* Unlimited
*Corporations:* Prohibited
*Unions:* Prohibited
*PACs:* Unlimited

### UTAH

*Individuals:* Unlimited
*Corporations:* Unlimited
*Unions:* Unlimited
*PACs:* Unlimited

### VERMONT

*Individuals:* $1,000/election
*Corporations:* $1,000/election
*Unions:* $1,000/election
*PACs:* $3,000/election

## VIRGINIA

*Individuals:* Unlimited
*Corporations:* Unlimited
*Unions:* Unlimited
*PACs:* Unlimited

## WASHINGTON

*Individuals:* $500/election for state legislative office,
$1,000/election for state executive office
*Corporations:* $500/election for state legislative office,
$1,000/election for state executive office
*Unions:* $500/election for state legislative office,
$1,000/election for state executive office
*PACs:* $500/election for state legislative office,
$1,000/election for state executive office

## WEST VIRGINIA

*Individuals:* $1,000/primary or general election
*Corporations:* Prohibited
*Unions:* $1,000/primary or general election
*PACs:* $1,000/primary or general election

## WISCONSIN

*Individuals:* State assembly: $500/year. State senate: $1,000/year. State-wide candidates: $10,000/year.
*Corporations:* Prohibited
*Unions:* Unions must establish PACs in order to give.
*PACs:* State assembly: $500/year. State senate: $1,000/year. State-wide candidates vary from $8,625 to $43,128/year depending on office.

## WYOMING

*Individuals:* $1,000/election
*Corporations:* Prohibited
*Unions:* Prohibited
*PACs:* Unlimited

## FEDERAL GOVERNMENT

*Individuals:* $1,000/election
*Corporations:* Prohibited, except through PACs
*Unions:* Prohibited, except through PACs
*PACs:* $5,000/election

# TRACKING
# THE MONEY

# 6

# GETTING STARTED

**G**etting to the bottom of the bottom line in political contributions can be a challenging and time-consuming task, but it's guaranteed to be a rewarding one. Even under the worst-case scenario — you're typing everything into the computer yourself, the contributors don't list their occupations or employers — you are guaranteed to learn things about the way politics works that you'd never have known without digging into the records.

While the process of hand-entering thousands of contribution records into a computer is no one's idea of a great way to pass the time, there is much to be said for the process of osmosis that inevitably occurs while you're doing it. The same names will pop up over and over again, as you begin to ferret out the top-spending lobbyists and other political rainmakers who are well-known to the politicians, yet all but unknown to anyone else. You'll see clusters of contributions from both expected and unexpected places. And, if you dig through enough records, you're almost guaranteed to find a scandal or two. Politicians are not always as careful at covering their financial tracks as one might think.

My own first experience at digging through campaign finance records was in Alaska in 1985. One of the most interesting discoveries was a cluster of $1,000 contributions to an incumbent state senator that all arrived the same day from an unlikely collection of givers. A total of $21,000 came in the door that day, from people none of the political reporters had ever heard of. They all lived in the Matanuska Valley, north of Anchorage, and they listed occupations like "farm hand," "construction worker," "potter" and, inevitably, a number of "homemakers" and "housewives."

Two of the contributions came from a husband-wife team. The woman owned a dairy, the man a construction company. Armed with the list of contributors and their addresses, I drove up to the valley to knock on doors. It didn't take long to find out the story. The contributions had all come from employees of this enterprising couple, and from the employees' spouses. As one contributor admitted to me — and later to a state inquiry — each employee was given a $1,500 "tool allowance" that was to be deposited in their personal checking accounts. They were then to write a $1,000 check to the senator, also from their personal checking accounts. The checks were then collected and hand delivered.

The dairy, it seemed, was nearing the deadline for complying with a state homesteading law that required a certain amount of work to be done to qualify for the homestead. They needed an extension or a waiver. The senator was in a position to recommend it. And so the $21,000 was rounded up and delivered.

The scam was uncovered simply by looking at campaign finance records, noticing a suspicious pattern — the similar amounts, the dates of the checks, the suspiciously blue-collar occupations of such big donors — and following up with old-fashioned legwork. The same kinds of stories, with local variations, are almost certainly buried in dusty filing cabinets from Olympia to Tallahassee and everywhere in between. All they await is someone digging into the records, systematically transferring the data from filing cabinets into a computer, then sifting through it to find what's there.

A number of other surprises were also uncovered in that initial investigation. A $20,000 bundle from a collection of apparently unconnected Seattle residents eventually was traced to an Alaska lobbyist acting on behalf of a Canadian corporation. (That one was caught because the givers used sequentially numbered cashier's checks to make their contributions. Alaska requires the check number to be recorded on each contribution.)

Then there were the recurring contributions from two Anchorage businessmen whose donations came not under their own names, but from 21 separate corporations they jointly owned. The contributions were typically for $250 each, but they were bundled — usually in groups of $1,000 or $2,000 — and delivered to favored candidates. When all the donations were added up, these two business partners turned out to be among the biggest contributors in Alaska. No one ever knew until we started digging through the filing cabinets, putting the contribution data on computer and sorting through it to see what we would find.

The same rewards await anyone who takes the time and effort to dig through the public records. From my own experience, and from that of other researchers who've dug through records on their own, I now recognize the symptoms of what happens when you begin to do this work. You work longer hours at the computer than you ever thought you would. Your eyes may be bloodshot, your fingers fighting off cramps, but there are few rewards so sweet as that adrenaline-pumping "bingo!" or "gotcha!" when a pattern jumps out at you, or the missing link in a seemingly unrelated collection of contributions suddenly falls into place. There's a lot to be said for the little discoveries you uncover simply through osmosis while sorting through the records. It's a nice reward for all the work.

Still, if you're going to try to dig out the facts behind who's underwriting the campaigns of your state legislature or city council or governor, there are many techniques, shortcuts and tools of the trade that will make the job easier and more fruitful. This section of the Handbook gives you the tools you'll need to get the job done.

## THE SEVEN STEPS

Before we get into the nuts and bolts of doing the job, it's worth an overview of what the job will consist of. Basically, there are seven major steps in identifying the money that pays for elections:

**1) Set the scope of your project and gather the records.** Are you looking to do the whole legislature? The governor's race? Your congressional delegation? Step one is figuring out how big your project will be, then gathering the records. To help get you started, the Handbook reviews on pages 59-69 what data is available in each of the 50 states and where to get it.

**2) Set up a database.** Next you have to get your computer ready to receive the data. Thankfully, nothing fancy is needed. Any off-the-shelf database program will do, and you can be up and running and ready to enter your records in less than an hour. There's no limit to the sophistication you can build into your database later if you want to, but for now all you need is a simple structure for holding the data you've collected.

**3) Enter and standardize the data.** If you're dealing with paper records, entering them into the computer will be your first big job. There are plenty of shortcuts that can help speed data entry, as well as things you should watch out for as you're progressing through the stacks of paper records. If you're importing records from a disk, or via modem, the data entry is already done and all you need to do is load it into your database. Either way, once the data is in, you'll need to clean up inconsistencies and standardize the names of contributors and their employers.

4) "Fingerprint" the contributors. This is the process of expanding the information you have on each contributor — assigning an ID number, filling in their occupation/employer or ideological interest, and identifying spouses and children who may also be contributing. The most time-consuming step here is identifying the contributors' occupations and/or employers. About half the states, and the federal government, require this information to be listed on contribution reports. If your state does, you're a giant step ahead in the fingerprinting process.

5) Categorize the contributions by industry and interest group. This is the step where you begin to hit paydirt. Instead of simply working with a list of names, companies and PACs, you'll now be classifying each contribution into its own industry or interest group category. Here's where you'll begin to see the real patterns — how much lawmakers are getting from dairy farmers, how much from lawyers and lobbyists, how much from the cable TV industry, securities brokers, public employee unions, or insurance executives. To do this, you'll need to do some digging in reference libraries, or plug in to one of the growing numbers of CD-ROMs that list companies by business type.

6) Look for patterns. Play with the data and see what you've got. This is the real fun. Now comes the time to sort through all the records, exploring what you've collected. Calculate the top political contributors in your state. Find out which industries have been targeting specific committees with generous helpings of campaign funds. Compile contributor profiles for key politicians, identifying their cash constituents whose identities were unknown before your research began.

7) Graph the most interesting patterns, and write your stories. After all the research, this is the time to put some flesh on the bones of your findings — doing the interviews, presenting the data in charts and graphs that will paint the picture so anyone can follow what is going on. Ideas on how to do this will come in Part III of the Handbook, "Reporting the Story." As for now, it's time for the nuts and bolts of how to get rolling.

# 7

# SETTING THE SCOPE OF YOUR RESEARCH

The first question facing you as you explore the possibilities of investigating money in politics is how big a chunk of contribution records you should try to examine. This question obviously depends on the resources you've got available — computer equipment, staffing, and time. It also depends on what state you're looking at. Categorizing all the contributions for the North Dakota legislature is one thing; doing it for California is quite another. No matter which state you examine, time and staffing are the crucial variables, since you can put together a database on virtually any computer you've got at your disposal. All you need is enough storage space on your hard drive, and just about any off-the-shelf database program. Even a spreadsheet will do for the data-entry part of the job if that's all you've got.

The ideal scope for a project would be a database that covers the entire state legislature, plus the governor and other top statewide elected officials. On a more local level, the entire city council is an obvious target, as are the candidates for mayor and, possibly, county commissioners. One way to cut down your workload is to restrict the research to only those candidates who were actually elected. You'll miss a lot of the money, clearly, but you'll have the most important data that you need when reporting on legislative issues. Another way to cut it — again, a compromise, but one to consider — is limiting your database to only those contributions over a certain amount, say $100 or $250 and above.

If the whole state legislature is too big a chunk to start with, a good way to pare down the scope of your project is to restrict it to one part of the legislature. You could do just the state senate or the house, you could concentrate on the house and senate leadership, or you could focus on one or a few key committees. If you can't take on the whole legislature, the next best thing is to do it by committee. Though voters rarely give it a thought, the real nuts and bolts work of the U.S. Congress, and most state legislatures, takes place at the committee level. In the Congress, and in the states, certain of those committees are important centers of power — and focal points for intensive lobbying and energetic contributions.

The House Ways and Means Committee, for example, which crafts the nation's tax laws, is crucial to virtually every business (and individual) in America. The Armed Services Committees and the Defense Appropriations Subcommittees can spell fiscal life or death for defense contractors. The House Energy and Commerce Committee — little known outside Washington — sets national policy for health care, telecommunications, the oil and gas industry, the securities and financial industries, electric utilities, railroads and a wide swath of other important industries. A seat on that committee, which virtually guarantees a generous supply of PAC contributions year after year, is one of the most sought-after assignments on Capitol Hill. Similar powerhouse committees exist in every state capitol. Focus your investigation on those committees and you will find the biggest centers of campaign funds in your state. You will likely also find the most direct correlations between campaign contributions and legislative actions. So if you can't do the whole legislature right away, start with a few top committees and expand your research later.

One important point on committees: if your state senators have longer terms than state house or assembly members (which almost every state does), *concentrate on the lower house first.* When lawmakers have to run every two years, their complete fundraising cycle will coincide with the normal two-year election cycle. In the U.S. Congress, where senators run only once every six years, you've got to look at a full six years of history (or three two-year election cycles) to get an accurate view of all the money going to a particular senate committee. Senators typically raise most of their money in the two years leading up to their reelection race, so if you review fundraising for the Senate Armed Services Committee in the 1992 election cycle, for example, you'll find that the biggest recipients of campaign cash were those with races in 1992. To get the full picture of who's been getting what you need to look back six full years. Keep that important point in mind as you begin your project. If you're doing your project committee-by-committee, it makes a lot more sense to start with the lower chamber and work up — particularly if you're short on time or resources.

## STRATEGIC ALLIANCES

This is a good a point to bring up a subject that ought to be considered as you're beginning to plan your project: is it important that you do it alone, or might it be possible to enter into a strategic alliance with another organization to help with the work? In some places, the competition between news organizations is so intense that the thought of a joint venture would be enough to scuttle the project outright. Two competing newspapers in the same city might be loathe to cooperate on anything, let alone on a database that could provide a rich lode of stories for months and years to come. But many other partnership possibilities may exist. Two Florida newspapers — the *Miami Herald* and the *St. Petersburg Times*— cooperated for a number of years in compiling a database of contributions to the Florida legislature. Other papers joined in at various times. Their readership areas, by and large, didn't overlap, and each paper successfully mined the database for unique stories.

Since ongoing analysis of the state legislature would probably be the highest priority in just about every state, similar cooperatives could be worked out almost anywhere, if the news organizations are willing to share resources.

Another possibility is teaming up with an academic or other non-profit research organization. A partnership with a university research group could provide a great deal of assistance to a news organization, as well as supplying rich material for class projects and case studies for the academics. You may well want to do a project on your own, but if you could use a hand with resources, and don't mind sharing at least a portion of your findings, don't rule out the idea of forming a partnership with another organization.

## SETTING UP A CONGRESSIONAL DATABASE

There's one other option you might want to consider, if the thought of entering thousands of records is too daunting — set up a database of contributors to congressional candidates. A logical slice here would be to include all the members of your state delegation, plus any current candidates. Frankly, this is something every news organization ought to have, both in its newsroom and its Washington bureau. It's also an excellent (and mostly painless) way to get started with a contributor database, since the data is already available electronically from the Federal Election Commission. Even better, you can get a database of contributions already coded into industry and interest group categories from the Center for Responsive Politics, or its affiliate, the National Library on Money & Politics.

The Center's coding process is not a quick one — we tend to be several months behind in PAC contributions and much longer behind in coding individuals — but at least all the work (or most of it, anyway) is already done. All you have to do is set up the database structure and import the records. The same is true of the FEC data (you just need to import the records), but the FEC doesn't standardize employers or apply category codes to PACs and individual contributions. Nevertheless, there's no data entry involved with a congressional database (unless you're trying to keep current with the latest election year filings), so the biggest single labor-intensive part of setting up the database is already done. Appendix B provides step-by-step instructions on downloading data from the FEC's on-line database.

# 8

## COLLECTING THE DATA

The starting point for your research will be the records available at the state, local, or federal agency that tracks the campaign contributions you're interested in. Since different jurisdictions have different disclosure laws — and since some offices are more computerized than others — there's a wide variance in what your actual starting point will be.

At worst — and this is the case in most states — you'll be dealing with paper records that have never been computerized. More and more states are beginning to put some of their contribution data on computer, and the federal government has done it for years. But most are still not there (and many will never be there due to budget constraints and a lack of interest) — all of which means your first job will be collecting copies of the paper records at the local office that handles them, and keying them into your computer by hand.

All the states have established prices for copying records, but keep in mind that these are designed for the typical customer who walks in the door — not for a news organization that wants not just a few reports, but whole filing cabinets full of records. Don't hesitate to try to negotiate a lower copy rate per page, or to bring your own paper — or even a portable copier — to their office. You might also try a little bartering — giving the office access to some of your data when you're done with it, or something else that's useful to them.

State elections offices are almost always in a delicate political position. They are invariably under-funded and overworked, their job is to regulate the very politicians who control their budget, and there are always pressures from lawmakers not to be too eager in their work. Nevertheless, nearly every office has one (or many) staffers who will be willing to bend over backwards to help you do the job that they themselves don't have the power or resources to do. Tap into those people, and every phase of your job will be easier.

## WHAT DATA DO YOU WANT TO COLLECT?

Your first question before beginning to collect the data for your research is figuring out exactly what data you need. There are two considerations here — what's available in your state and how big a chunk you can bite off without being overwhelmed.

In every state, candidates for public office must file periodic reports of the money coming into their campaign and going out of it in expenditures. The records you're interested in (at least for the scope of research outlined in this book) is the money coming in — the contributions received.

When candidates file their reports, they list two specific kinds of information. On the summary page of their report, they'll list the totals — how much money has come in to their campaign in the last reporting period, and how much they've spent. Typically, they also include additional information, such as the candidate's current cash on hand, and the running totals of their contributions and expenditures over the past year. These summary pages are valuable in their own right, particularly when you're writing election season stories under tight deadlines. They offer a quick comparison showing the amounts raised by different candidates, and they're often used to informally handicap who the "serious" candidates are. But for researching the *source* of the campaign funds, you can skip the summaries for now and go straight to the detail pages.

In every state candidates must itemize all contributions over a certain amount. The threshold varies from state to state. At the federal level, all contributions of $200 or more must be itemized. In a few states, *all* contributions must be itemized. But in most, contributions smaller than the threshold amount can be reported simply in lump sum.

*The part of the reports that you're interested in are the itemized contributions.* Each of these entries will typically include the name, address, and sometimes the occupation of the contributor, as well as the amount given and the date of the contribution. That information is the core of what you'll be putting into your database.

## STARTING POINTS FOR COLLECTING DATA:
## A STATE-BY-STATE ROUNDUP

To help get you started in planning your project, the listings below review some essential information you'll need to know, in each of the 50 states. Each listing includes the following information:

• The phone number of the agency that oversees the collection of campaign finance reports.

• Fees charged for copying reports. Take this as your starting point, since some offices may let you cut this cost by bringing in your own copier and doing the work yourself, or by supplying your own paper.

• The threshold for itemizing contributions. Any contributions below this amount are reported only in the aggregate. Contributions above the threshold must be listed individually. These itemized contributions are the ones you'll be entering into your database.

• Occupation/employer requirements. Twenty-seven states currently require candidates to provide information on the occupation and employer of their contributors. Of all the elements you'll be entering into your database, this is the most important, since it's the key to finding out the economic interests of contributors. If your state does not require this information, you'll have to find it out independently — a much more difficult job, though not impossible. (One saving grace in case your state does not require this information — it's relevant only to contributions from individuals. Corporate, union and PAC contributions can be classified simply by looking up the name of the contributor, as in Crazy Joe's Used Car Sales, or the local Realtors Association.)

• The availability, if any, of electronic data on campaign contributions. Obviously, if you're looking to investigate a state that's already put some of its data on computer — even if it's from a previous election cycle — you're that much farther ahead in compiling your own database. Don't hesitate to collect everything you can that's already computerized.

### ALABAMA
205-242-7210
*Copying cost per page:* $1.00
*Threshold for itemizing:* Over $100
*Occupation/employer required:* No
*Electronic data available:* Summary data only on-line (total receipts & expenditures). Call to get password.

## ALASKA

907-276-4176

*Copying cost per page:* Do-it-yourself for 25¢ page. If the office does it, cost is free for first 10 pages, then 20¢/page — but you may have to wait a few days for copies.

*Threshold for itemizing:* Over $100

*Occupation/employer required:* Yes. Check number must also be included.

*Electronic data available:* Contributions & expenditures are available online (and on disk) for 1990 statewide races, 1991 municipal & statewide races, and some races in 1992. Nothing has been added since 1992. Contributions from the 1990 elections (and partial data from 1992) are available on disk from the Western States Center. Phone 406-449-8878.

## ARIZONA

602-542-8683

*Copying cost per page:* 50¢

*Threshold for itemizing:* Over $25

*Occupation/employer required:* Yes

*Electronic data available:* Candidates' contributions & expenditures are available on disk. Total contributions from PACs are also available. Cost is $25 for non-commercial users plus $5/disk. Data from 1990-present.

## ARKANSAS

501-682-5070

*Copying cost per page:* 80¢

*Threshold for itemizing:* $100 & above

*Occupation/employer required:* Yes

*Electronic data available:* None

## CALIFORNIA

916-322-4880

*Copying cost per page:* 10¢

*Threshold for itemizing:* $100 or more/year

*Occupation/employer required:* Yes

*Electronic data available:* None from the state itself. Legitech, a subsidiary of McClatchy Newspapers, does pick up the reports and provide computerized listings of contributions for both incumbents and challengers — though at a premium price. Their phone number is 916-447-1886. Data is available online dating back to 1987. Subscriptions for the online service are available at $175/hr if you purchase two hours of online time, or $150/hr if you sign up for eight hours.

## COLORADO

303-894-2680

*Copying cost per page:* 50¢

*Threshold for itemizing:* Over $25

*Occupation/employer required:* No

*Electronic data available:* "In the works" beginning (hopefully) fall 1994.

## CONNECTICUT

203-566-3059

*Copying cost per page:* 50¢

*Threshold for itemizing:* Over $30

*Occupation/employer required:* Yes, for contributions over $1,000, otherwise only name & address. In both cases, donor must disclose whether he/she is a lobbyist or a lobbyist's spouse or dependent. Donors of over $1,000 must additionally disclose whether they or their business have any state contracts valued at more than $5,000.

*Electronic data available:* None

## DELAWARE

302-739-4277

*Copying cost per page:* 25¢

*Threshold for itemizing:* Over $100

*Occupation/employer required:* No

*Electronic data available:* None

## FLORIDA

904-488-7697

*Copying cost per page:* 15¢ single-sided, 20¢ double-sided

*Threshold for itemizing:* Over $100

*Occupation/employer required:* Yes, for contributions over $100, otherwise only name & address.

*Electronic data available:* Itemized contributions to gubernatorial and cabinet candidates are available on a nine-track computer tape. Cost is $25 plus postage.

## GEORGIA

404-656-2871

*Copying cost per page:* 25¢

*Threshold for itemizing:* $101 or more

*Occupation/employer required:* Yes

*Electronic data available:* None

## HAWAII

808-586-0285

*Copying cost per page:* 25¢

*Threshold for itemizing:* Over $100

*Occupation/employer required:* No

*Electronic data available:* Access via Internet (ABLDOM@HINC.HAWAII.GOV). Online listing of contributions, expenditures & other data for 1990 and 1992; 1994 data will follow later. Data is also available on disk.

## IDAHO

208-334-2852

*Copying cost per page:* 25¢

*Threshold for itemizing:* Over $50

*Occupation/employer required:* No

*Electronic data available:* Contributions available on disk for last two elections. Cost is $25/disk. Contributions from the 1990 and 1992 elections are also available on disk from the Western States Center. Phone 406-449-8878.

## ILLINOIS

217-782-4141

*Copying cost per page:* 25¢ for paper records, 50¢ for microfiche (60 pages per 4x6 sheet — but you need a microfiche reader to decipher it).

*Threshold for itemizing:* Over $150

*Occupation/employer required:* No

*Electronic data available:* None

NOTE: Anyone requesting copies of contribution reports must fill out a D-3 request form for each report, listing your name, occupation, employer and reason for viewing the report. A copy is sent to the candidate whose report was examined.

## INDIANA

317-232-3939

*Copying cost per page:* 15¢, or 5¢ if you supply the paper

*Threshold for itemizing:* Over $100

*Occupation/employer required:* No

*Electronic data available:* Online listing of summary data for 1994, available only on in-house terminal. You can get printouts of this, but nothing on disk.

## IOWA

515-281-4411

*Copying cost per page:* 15¢ in the office, 35¢ on phone orders, $1/page if report is faxed to you.

*Threshold for itemizing:* Over $25

*Occupation/employer required:* No

*Electronic data available:* None

## KANSAS

913-296-4561

*Copying cost per page:* 25¢

*Threshold for itemizing:* Over $50

*Occupation/employer required:* Yes, for contributions of $150 or above, otherwise only name & address.

*Electronic data available:* Itemized contributions from the 1994 election cycle are available on disk, but they're costly. The office recommends getting data from Information Network of Kansas (1-800-452-6727), though that's not cheap, either. Network membership is $50/year. On-line connect time to access the contribution records is 40¢/minute.

## KENTUCKY

502-573-2226
*Copying cost per page:* 10¢ plus postage
*Threshold for itemizing:* Over $100
*Occupation/employer required:* Yes
*Electronic data available:* In 1994, for the first time, candidates for governor & lieutenant governor are filing electronically. Disks of their contribution reports are available.

## LOUISIANA

504-765-2308
*Copying cost per page:* 25¢
*Threshold for itemizing:* ALL contributions
*Occupation/employer required:* No
*Electronic data available:* None

## MAINE

207-287-6219
*Copying cost per page:* 20¢ plus postage
*Threshold for itemizing:* Over $50
*Occupation/employer required:* Yes
*Electronic data available:* None

## MARYLAND

410-974-3711
*Copying cost per page:* 15¢/page in the office, phone orders 25¢/page plus $7 per hour plus postage
*Threshold for itemizing:* Over $50
*Occupation/employer required:* No
*Electronic data available:* None

## MASSACHUSETTS

617-727-8352
*Copying cost per page:* 10¢/page in the office. Phone or mail orders: 20¢/page plus approximately $11 per hour plus postage
*Threshold for itemizing:* Over $50
*Occupation/employer required:* Beginning in 1995, contributors who give over $200 must disclose their occupation/employer.
*Electronic data available:* None

## MICHIGAN

517-373-2540

*Copying cost per page:* 22¢/page if they copy. If you copy, cost is 3¢/page for single-sided, 4¢ for double-sided, 5¢ off the microfiche.

*Threshold for itemizing:* Over $20

*Occupation/employer required:* Yes, for contributions over $200, otherwise only name & address.

*Electronic data available:* Contribution data for 1994 is beginning to be available on disk, as the office key-punches the reports.

## MINNESOTA

612-296-5148

*Copying cost per page:* 25¢/page in-house, $1/page for phone orders

*Threshold for itemizing:* Over $100

*Occupation/employer required:* Yes

*Electronic data available:* None

## MISSISSIPPI

601-359-1350

*Copying cost per page:* 50¢/page, 25¢/page in-house

*Threshold for itemizing:* Over $500 for statewide & supreme court candidates, over $200 for others

*Occupation/employer required:* Yes

*Electronic data available:* None yet. As of late summer 1994 they were "just about through" entering records for 1991-92.

## MISSOURI

314-751-2020 or 1-800-392-8660

*Copying cost per page:* 10¢/page

*Threshold for itemizing:* Over $100

*Occupation/employer required:* No

*Electronic data available:* None

## MONTANA

406-444-2942

*Copying cost per page:* 10¢

*Threshold for itemizing:* $35 & above

*Occupation/employer required:* Yes

*Electronic data available:* None from the state, but contributions from the 1990 and 1992 elections are available on disk from the Western States Center. Phone 406-449-8878.

## NEBRASKA

402-471-2522
*Copying cost per page:* 50¢
*Threshold for itemizing:* Over $100
*Occupation/employer required:* No
*Electronic data available:* Contributions are available on disk for the 1990 and 1992 elections.

## NEVADA

702-687-3176
*Copying cost per page:* 50¢
*Threshold for itemizing:* Over $500
*Occupation/employer required:* No
*Electronic data available:* None from the state, but contributions from the 1990 and 1992 elections are available on disk from the Western States Center. Phone 406-449-8878.

## NEW HAMPSHIRE

603-271-3242
*Copying cost per page:* 25¢
*Threshold for itemizing:* Over $25
*Occupation/employer required:* Yes, for contributions over $100, otherwise only name & address
*Electronic data available:* None.

## NEW JERSEY

609-292-8700
*Copying cost per page:* First 10 pages 50¢/page, next 10 pages 25¢/page, then 15¢/page
*Threshold for itemizing:* Over $200
*Occupation/employer required:* Yes
*Electronic data available:* Contributions for all legislative and gubernatorial candidates for 1985-91 elections are available. Cost is $125 per mainframe tape. Data is also available on diskettes, but cost is $125/disk, so mainframe tapes are the only economical alternative.

## NEW MEXICO

505-827-3620
*Copying cost per page:* 25¢
*Threshold for itemizing:* ALL contributions
*Occupation/employer required:* Yes, for contributions of $250 & above, otherwise only name & address
*Electronic data available:* Online listing of contributions and expenditures for 1994. Available only on in-house terminal.

### NEW YORK

518-474-8200 or 1-800-458-3453 in NY state
*Copying cost per page:* 25¢
*Threshold for itemizing:* Over $99
*Occupation/employer required:* No
*Electronic data available:* None from the state itself. Legitech, a subsidiary of McClatchy Newspapers, does pick up the reports and provide computerized listings (at a premium price), but only for incumbents. Their number is 518-434-2242. Data is available online dating back to 1985. Subscriptions for the online data are available at $175/hr if you purchase two hours of online time, or $150/hr if you sign up for eight hours.

### NORTH CAROLINA

919-733-2186
*Copying cost per page:* 25¢/page if they copy. 10¢/page if you copy in the office.
*Threshold for itemizing:* Over $100
*Occupation/employer required:* No
*Electronic data available:* Contributions for all statewide candidates are available for 1989-94. No charge if you bring your own pre-formatted diskettes.

### NORTH DAKOTA

701-224-3660
*Copying cost per page:* 25¢
*Threshold for itemizing:* Over $100
*Occupation/employer required:* No
*Electronic data available:* None

### OHIO

614-466-2585
*Copying cost per page:* $1 for first page, then 10¢/page
*Threshold for itemizing:* All contributions are itemized, except individual contributions of $25 or less made at a fundraiser.
*Occupation/employer required:* No
*Electronic data available:* Contributions for statewide candidates from 1990. Cost is $5/disk.

### OKLAHOMA

405-521-3451
*Copying cost per page:* 25¢/page. $1/page if report is faxed.
*Threshold for itemizing:* Over $50
*Occupation/employer required:* Yes
*Electronic data available:* Contributions to statewide candidates in 1992, some for 1990. Free if you bring your own diskettes.

## OREGON

503-986-1518

*Copying cost per page:* 25¢
*Threshold for itemizing:* Over $100 statewide/over $50 other
*Occupation/employer required:* Yes
*Electronic data available:* None from the state, but contributions from the 1990 and 1992 elections are available on disk from the Western States Center. Phone 406-449-8878.

## PENNSYLVANIA

717-787-5280

*Copying cost per page:* 10¢
*Threshold for itemizing:* $50 or over
*Occupation/employer required:* Yes, for contributions over $250, otherwise only name & address
*Electronic data available:* None

## RHODE ISLAND

401-277-2056

*Copying cost per page:* 15¢
*Threshold for itemizing:* Over $100
*Occupation/employer required:* Yes
*Electronic data available:* At the end of every year, the state publishes a book of all contributors who gave over $100 to any candidate. The 1993 book costs $20. The book is also available on disk for the same price.

## SOUTH CAROLINA

803-253-4192

*Copying cost per page:* 20¢
*Threshold for itemizing:* Over $100
*Occupation/employer required:* No
*Electronic data available:* None

## SOUTH DAKOTA

605-773-3537

*Copying cost per page:* 30¢/page for first 10 pages, then 10¢/page
*Threshold for itemizing:* Over $100
*Occupation/employer required:* Yes
*Electronic data available:* None

## TENNESSEE

615-741-7959

*Copying cost per page:* 25¢/page if they copy. 10¢/page if you copy.
*Threshold for itemizing:* Over $100
*Occupation/employer required:* No
*Electronic data available:* None

## TEXAS

512-463-5800

*Copying cost per page:* 12¢

*Threshold for itemizing:* Over $50 per period

*Occupation/employer required:* No

*Electronic data available:* Online listing of contributions and expenditures and other information for statewide candidates for current election. Available on Texas Ethics Commission BBS at 512-458-9424 or 1-800-227-8392 (State Comptroller's Window on State Government BBS). Free except for phone toll charges. Also available on disk at $1/disk.

## UTAH

801-538-1040

*Copying cost per page:* 20¢/page if you copy in office (10¢/page if you bring paper). 35¢/page if they copy.

*Threshold for itemizing:* Over $50

*Occupation/employer required:* No

*Electronic data available:* Detailed contribution reports are available on disk, but only for PACs. The disk costs $47.50. Contributions from the 1990 elections are available on disk from the Western States Center. Phone 406-449-8878.

## VERMONT

802-828-2363

*Copying cost per page:* 2¢

*Threshold for itemizing:* Over $100

*Occupation/employer required:* No

*Electronic data available:* None

## VIRGINIA

804-786-6551

*Copying cost per page:* 25¢

*Threshold for itemizing:* Over $100

*Occupation/employer required:* Yes. Requirement to list occupation/employer began July 1, 1993.

*Electronic data available:* None

## WASHINGTON

206-753-1111

*Copying cost per page:* 25¢ plus postage for copies of microfiche

*Threshold for itemizing:* Over $25

*Occupation/employer required:* Yes, for contributions over $100, otherwise only name & address

*Electronic data available:* Summary data on candidates' contributions is available online by calling the state's online Magic System at 206-664-2222. You'll need a copy of PC Anywhere to connect. The public disclosure office

also has an address on the Internet:  PDC@OLYMPUS.DIS.WA.GOV.
Contributions from the 1990 and 1992 elections are available on disk from
the Western States Center. Phone 406-449-8878.

## WEST VIRGINIA

304-558-6000
*Copying cost per page:* $1 for first page, then 75¢/page
*Threshold for itemizing:* ALL contributions
*Occupation/employer required:* Yes, for contributions over $250, other-
wise only name.
*Electronic data available:* None

## WISCONSIN

608-266-8005
*Copying cost per page:* 20¢
*Threshold for itemizing:* Over $20
*Occupation/employer required:* Yes, for contributions over $100, other-
wise only name & address
*Electronic data available:* None

## WYOMING

307-777-7186
*Copying cost per page:* 50¢/page for first 10 pages, then 15¢/page
*Threshold for itemizing:* $25 & above
*Occupation/employer required:* No. Contributors also do not need to list
their street address, only their city.
*Electronic data available:*  Contributions for statewide and legislative
candidates for 1990 and 1992 are both available on disk. Cost is $115 for
both election cycles. Data from those election cycles is also available from
the Western States Center. Phone 406-449-8878.

# 9

# SETTING UP A DATABASE
# AND ENTERING DATA

omputer-assisted reporting is a hot-button topic around newsrooms
these days. Some news organizations have made computer-assisted reporting a major priority, and are using mainframes, nine-track tapes
and powerful PCs to investigate areas that previously were untouchable. Many
others have yet to step into the computer age beyond using terminals for word
processing. Most are probably somewhere in between.

The good news about campaign finance databases is that they are among
the easiest of all database projects to set up. In fact, putting together a do-it-
yourself contributor database is so simple technically that it's the ideal project
to get a reporter — or a whole news organization — up and comfortable with
computer databases.

Anyone, with even the smallest of computers and the most rudimentary
of database programs, can put together a database. No fancy equipment is
needed, and the work can be done (if there's no support from editors) in odd
hours of the day, or nights and weekends.

Organizations wanting to jump in in a big way can build as sophisticated
a database as you could dream of with an industrial-strength program such as

FoxPro, Paradox, or the newer generation of programs such as Microsoft Access. If you know your way around databases, pick whichever program you're most comfortable with. If you don't know a database from a spreadsheet, *find the simplest, most intuitive program you can*, and set it up in that. You shouldn't have to pay more than about $100 for a simple "flat-file" database. For more sophisticated systems, a "relational" database is ideal. *But it's not necessary, particularly when you're getting started.* Better to learn as you go using a simpler, more intuitive program, then move on to something bigger if and when you need to. (Once the data is in the computer, it's a relatively simple matter to transfer it from one program to another.)

If you're going to be hand-entering printed data into your database (which you'll likely have to do if you're looking at state or municipal records), pick a program that offers shortcuts for data entry. If you're using a Macintosh, Panorama is an excellent choice.

### A FEW WORDS FOR NON-TECHNICAL READERS . . .

If you're a computer neophyte or computerphobe, this may be the point where you're beginning to work yourself into a nervous sweat. Don't worry. Amazing advances have been made in recent years in making computers much more friendly than they've ever been before. As a longtime Macintosh user, I long ago got used to the notion that computers ought to make life easier, not more complicated, and that software ought to be intuitive enough that you hardly need to open the manual to figure it out. Thankfully, this trend toward simplicity, and away from the mind-boggling complexities of years past, has swept beyond Macs into the PC-compatible world as well. Microsoft Windows has been the primary carrier, and though it's not yet as simple and elegant as the Mac, it's getting closer all the time.

The current crop of database programs make data entry, and development of simple, yet powerful databases infinitely easier than they were a few years ago. Entering campaign contribution data into a database is about the easiest thing you can do to get your feet wet in this brave new world. It will allow you to ease in slowly. Once you dip your toe in, you'll find the water's fine.

### STRUCTURE OF THE DATABASE

Database programs allow you to take huge amounts of data and store them in your computer piece by piece, so you can rearrange them easily, sort through them, calculate totals, and basically manipulate them in almost any way imaginable. To do it, databases break up the data into individual records and "fields." A *record* is a single transaction — a contribution to a state senate candidate, for example. A *field* is an element within that record, such as the contributor's name, the amount of the contribution, the date, etc.

To set up your first campaign finance database, you should begin with the paper records and set up the computer to mimic those forms. The records you're primarily interested in are the itemized contributions to candidates. These records will typically include the contributor's name and address, the candidate's name, and the amount and date of the contribution. Each of these elements should be fields in your database.

About half the states, and the federal government, also require contributions over a threshold amount to include the contributor's occupation and employer. Of all the bits of data, this is probably the most important, since it's the one you'll use later to assign an industry or interest group code to the contribution. If your state requires this information, be sure to include extra fields for them in your database.

A handful of states require additional information. If yours does, you'll want to add that as another field, too. Alaska, for example, requires candidates to write down the check number of each contribution over $100 — a useful idea that makes it possible to identify connections between contributors that are not otherwise visible. Connecticut requires contributors to reveal whether they are lobbyists, or members of a lobbyist's immediate family. Kentucky requires statewide candidates to disclose the name and employer of the contributor's spouse (an excellent way of identifying the economic interests behind what otherwise would be a contribution from a "housewife" or "homemaker"). Obviously, these extra bits of information are valuable — if the forms you're looking at include them, be sure to include them as extra fields in your database.

Let's assume you have all the standard elements on the paper records you're working with. Here's a workable structure you can use to get started.

| Data | Field name | Length | Field type |
|------|-----------|--------|-----------|
| Contributor's name | Contname | 40 | Character |
| Contributor type | Conttype | 1 | Character |
| Candidate's name | Candname | 20 | Character |
| Contributor's address | Address | 40 | Character |
| Contributor's city | City | 18 | Character |
| Contributor's state | State | 2 | Character |
| Contributor's zip | Zip | 5 | Character |
| Contributor's occupation | Occupation | 30 | Character |
| Contributor's employer | Employer | 40 | Character |
| Contribution date | Date | 8 | Date |
| Amount | Amount | 5 | Numeric |

Later you'll be adding extra fields — ID numbers for contributors and candidates, a "newemploy" field to hold the contributors' standardized employer/occupation, and a code that lets you classify the contribution by a specific industry or interest group. Don't worry about those fields now. First you need to get the records into your computer, and the simple setup outlined above is all you need. Once you've got your database structure, you're ready to start entering data.

A few comments on some of the fields are in order here:

**Contributor's name.** The traditional way to store names in computer databases is to break the name up into at least two, and possibly several fields: first name, last name, middle initial, prefix, suffix, etc. Are all these fields really necessary? Based on my own experience at working with these databases, I'd give a qualified no. It might be useful to have a first name-last name division, but even that's not really necessary — and there's at least one compelling reason why it's better to keep it all as a single field. Many of the contributors you'll be entering are not individuals, but organizations — whether PACs, unions, or corporations. Fitting their full name into the "lastname" field is going to be difficult, unless you make the lastname field 40 characters long. (And if you do that, you'll be using up lots of unnecessary disk space.) If you find you later do need two fields, you can always create them by having the computer split them apart. It's also more convenient to sort on a single field than on two fields.

If you do enter contributor names as a single field, do it in the following format: "Jones, Henry B Jr" (or Dr, or MD, etc). You'll be sorting the names later alphabetically, so make sure the last name comes first, followed by a comma, followed by the first name and any other initials or professional abbreviations.

### TIPS WHEN ENTERING NAMES

• When you're entering names, don't forget extra elements like "Jr", "Sr", "Dr", "Mrs," etc. Also be sure to include any extra initials at the end, like "MD", "DDS", "CPA," etc. that will help you identify their occupation.

• Do *not* copy "Mr." or "Ms." into your database, and if you're starting out with records that are already computerized, strip away the "Mr." from the files. This will help you later when you're trying to standardize names. On the other hand, *do* copy "Mrs." — particularly if the name is a man's, as in "Mrs. Henry Jones."

• Eliminate periods after abbreviations like "Mrs.," "Dr.," etc. and also after middle initials. It's just an extra keystroke and it doesn't tell you anything you don't already know.

• Be consistent when entering names of people with two first initials. Probably the easiest is to leave a space, but no periods, between the two initials, as in "H R Haldeman." Once you start doing it this way, don't switch to "HR Haldeman," or the records won't be line up alphabetically when you start sorting.

**Contributor type.** Later, it will be useful to separate individuals from other types of contributors. Enter a one-letter code here to tell yourself what kind of contributor this is. You don't need to get too specific. The following codes will do:

P = PAC. Political action committee.
I = Individual.
C = Corporation or other business organization.
L = Labor union.
R = Republican Party, and its local affiliates.
D = Democratic Party, and its local affiliates.
3 = Other political parties.

These will be useful later. You'll want to isolate the individuals, for example, to standardize their names, search for spouses, and arrange them by occupation/employer.

**Candidate's name.** Since you'll be entering a block of records from a single candidate at a time, it will be easier not to fill in the candidate's name for every record. Rather, leave this field blank as you're going through a report, then enter them all with a single computer command when you come to the end of the candidate. An even better option, if your database allows it, is to set up the candidate name as a default that's automatically entered into each new record as you create it. When you move to a new candidate, you change the default to the new name, and proceed as before. Another point: this field doesn't have to include the candidate's full name. There are far fewer candidates than contributors, and you generally know who they are. So enter only as much as you really need to — Rostenkowski or Smith, Bob is likely to be sufficient.

**Contributor's address.** This is the street address of the contributor. It's likely to be one of the most complicated and time-consuming fields to enter, but it will be very useful later when you're trying to link spouses and children with the income-earner in the family.

• You don't really need to enter the address every single time, particularly if the contributor is a PAC, since you won't need the PAC's address to identify it later. If the contributor is a corporation, however, its address may well be useful, as executives from the company sometimes list their office address on personal contributions. (This also helps you confirm their place of employment in case they don't list it.)

• Eliminate periods. Abbreviate wherever you can, and be consistent. Use "PO Box" instead of "Post Office Box" or "P. O. Box." Every keystroke saved is a keystroke closer to finishing the job.

**Contributor's city, state and zip.** These are three separate fields. They'll be useful for a variety of things later — like determining in-state vs. out-of-state contribution totals, for example, or compiling a list of the golden zip codes with the deepest political pockets. The city and state fields in particular are ones that will be repeated over and over again, so look for a database program that will allow you to "repeat" the entry from the previous record automatically. (In other words, if you've got 25 contributions in a row from "Los Angeles," let the computer fill it in when you tab to the city field. Other programs (like Panorama on the Mac) have a feature they call "clairvoyance." You type the first two or three letters of the word and it fills in the rest, based on what you filled in earlier in that field. Another thing you can do is skip the field as you're entering the records, then fill in a block of them later, through cutting and pasting or a simple replicate command. Yet another option is using temporary abbreviations — LA for Los Angeles, for example, or Chi for Chicago. When you're all finished, it's easy to have the computer expand these abbreviations to the full word.

**Contributor's occupation/employer.** The federal government requires that this information be listed on all contributions of $200 or more. Many states also require it, though the dollar threshold for disclosing it varies. Of all the fields in your database, this one is probably the most important. It will be the basis of your calculations on who the biggest contributors are, and which industries give most heavily. This is also the field you'll be concentrating on when the time comes to assign category codes to each contribution.

### *TIPS WHEN ENTERING EMPLOYER/OCCUPATION NAMES*

• Abbreviate whenever possible, and be consistent. Use "Inc" and "Corp" and "Co" and don't use periods.

• Replace "and" with "&" as in "Jones & Day" or "Ferrari & Sons Construction."

• Law firms pose a special challenge, as they usually consist of a string of names, as in "Akin, Gump, Strauss, Hauer & Feld." The rule of thumb we use at the Center, and one we recommend, is including the full name of the firm *only if there are three or fewer names in it.* For anything longer, use the first two names and "et al" — as in "Akin, Gump et al." It's shorter that way, and it's also more consistent, as law firms have a way of changing their names as partners come and go. (The first couple of names in the law firm usually stay the same, but the latter names often vary through the years.)

• Be consistent in how you treat names of companies that begin with initials. In general, it's best **not** to use spaces between the initials. Use "EF Hutton, " for example, not "E F Hutton" or "AT&T," not "A T & T." But whatever you do, don't mix and match the styles, or your records won't match up when they're sorted later. And again, save keystrokes and don't use periods.

**Date of the contribution.** Most database programs allow you to easily format a date field so you need to type only a few characters of the date, not the whole thing. Since most of the contributions will at least be from the same year, you can use these formatting features, type something like 0512 and have the computer fill out the date automatically as "5/12/94." Again, the important thing is to eliminate keystrokes wherever possible.

**Amount of the contribution.** This is a numeric field, formatted in dollars. Don't bother with cents at all — just enter $500 for a contribution of that amount, not $500.00. If you come across any contributions for odd amounts, like $259.95, round it off to $260.

Because many of the fields will be repeating themselves in a given series of records — the same city or state or candidate, for example — it makes a lot of sense to set up your computer screen in a row-and-column spreadsheet-type format, rather than as individual records. You could even use a spreadsheet program to enter the data, then transfer it later into a database.

One final word on entering data. The temptation, after you've entered your last record, is to get on to the next step (or to turn off the computer and go home). But your work is not quite finished. *This is the time to go back and proof your work, comparing the computer records with the paper records.* Your accuracy will be better (and your eyes will be healthier) if you print out your records rather than scanning them quickly on the computer screen. If the paper reports have subtotals on every page, recheck your own totals to make sure they match.

Long hours of data entry is no one's idea of a good time, but it's a necessary first step in computerizing campaign finance data. Who should do it? The reporter who's organizing the project? Temp workers? Student interns? The choice will likely depend on budgetary factors — both financial and timewise.

As long as you carefully check the records once they're in, there is no reason not to let someone else help you input the data. If you're fortunate enough to be able to hire temporary employees, terrific. If you're able to round up a few volunteers from around the newsroom — other reporters or interns — that's fine too. Just be sure everyone is using the same stylistic conventions, the same abbreviations, and the same penchant for detail and accuracy.

Whatever the arrangement, the one recommendation I would have is that the reporter who is doing the main work should be one of the people inputting the data. If you can find someone to help you, great. But even if you do get help, it's important to get your hands dirty in entering data yourself. The most important reason is osmosis. You simply pick things up — trends, names that keep repeating, oddities that bear further investigation — subtle things that tell you something is going on that looks a little suspect. The other thing hands-on inputting does is give you a sense of what everybody else is doing. It's tough to supervise someone on a job you've never really done yourself. Be a participant, even if you do have the luxury of supervising a team of inputters rather than doing it all yourself.

The ideal situation for a news organization tackling the job of trying to computerize, say, the campaign finance records of an entire state legislature, would be to form a strategic alliance with another organization, such as a local university or university-sponsored research organization. This is a project that would make an ideal classroom project in political science, journalism, or both. It would help bring the real world of politics into the theoretical world of the classroom, and it would provide an education for all involved. It would also provide enough extra help for news organizations that it could make the difference in actually convincing your editors or publisher to undertake a major project.

As long as the work is supervised, as long as accuracy and consistency can be insured, it doesn't really matter who puts the paper records into the computer. It only matters that it gets done, because once those records are in electronic format, the real fun begins.

# 10

## STANDARDIZING THE DATA

To make computers do what they do best, inconsistencies in real-world data need to be smoothed out. That's the situation you're facing when dealing with thousands of campaign contribution records that have been filled in by hand by dozens of campaign treasurers and aides. Names of contributors, and the companies they work for, will have almost endless variations. What you need to do once you've got the raw data in your computer is to standardize the names. Is John H. Jeffords the same as J. H. Jeffords or Jack Jeffords? For that matter, was John T. Jeffords a different person, or just a misprint? You can nearly always tell by checking the wider context.

Before you start standardizing, though, you've got to add two new fields to your database — a contributor ID and a "newemploy" field:

| Data | Field name | Length | Field type |
|------|-----------|--------|-----------|
| Contributor ID | ContribID | 9 | Character |
| Occupation/employer | Newemploy | 40 | Character |

The contributor ID has a length of nine characters. The Federal Election Commission uses a nine-digit code to identify candidates and PACs, so your database will be able to accommodate those codes directly if you use nine characters too. You probably will never need that many characters in a database under a million records, but the space can actually come in handy. You can have the computer generate a sequence of numbers, but my own advice would be to generate the ID based on two factors — the first three letters of the contributor's last name and then a five-digit sequential number. Don't worry if the numerical part of the ID isn't perfectly sorted alphabetically. It doesn't have to be; in the beginning, it only needs to be unique *for each contribution.* As you go through the contributor names alphabetically, finding multiple contributions from the same person, you'll replace all those unique IDs with a single ID for each contributor.

To do that, you've first got to sort all the contributor names alphabetically. Line 'em up, Aaron through Zuchelli. Last name, followed by a comma, followed by the first name, as in "Maloney, Richard B." This is the simplest way to find identical, or nearly identical, names. When you find two names that are identical –- or close matches with the same address — give them the same ID number. Here's how it works:

*Original list:*

| Contributor | Amount | Date | Candidate | ContribID |
|---|---|---|---|---|
| Jones, Henrietta | $250 | 4/12/94 | Calhoun | JON21929 |
| Jones, Henrietta | $500 | 9/4/94 | Wilson | JON39299 |
| Jones, Henrietta | $500 | 9/14/94 | Emerson | JON39321 |
| Jones, Henrietta | $250 | 11/1/94 | Emerson | JON40032 |

Since the contributor is the same in each case, you take the first ID number and copy it to all the other contributions made by the same person:

*Revised list:*

| Contributor | Amount | Date | Candidate | ContribID |
|---|---|---|---|---|
| Jones, Henrietta | $250 | 4/12/94 | Calhoun | JON21929 |
| Jones, Henrietta | $500 | 9/4/94 | Wilson | JON21929 |
| Jones, Henrietta | $500 | 9/14/94 | Emerson | JON21929 |
| Jones, Henrietta | $250 | 11/1/94 | Emerson | JON21929 |

It doesn't really matter which of the original contributor ID's you choose to duplicate. All that matters is that every contribution from Henrietta Jones is identified with the same ID.

You can skip the letters and use eight numbers if you want, but you do need to limit the ID to eight characters, because you're going to be adding a ninth character to some contributors later. That ninth character will be used to designate non-income-earning family members after you've connected them to the person in the household who brings home the bacon.

If Henrietta Jones, from the example above, had a non-income-earning husband named Clyde, his ID would become JON21929A. If Henrietta and Clyde had a 12-year-old daughter named Eunice, her ID would be JON21929B. This coding system also makes it easy to keep up with the Joneses if they multiply. Any other children who come along later (and give contributions) can be added simply by adding a C, D, E, etc. to the original eight-digit ID. And all would be linked to Henrietta, since she's the one in the family who earns the income.

There are a number of reasons why a contributor ID makes sense, but its biggest benefit is that it allows you to link related (and identical) contributors regardless of any variations in the name you find on the contribution reports. Henrietta Jones may show up in your database with any number of variations in her name — whether due to nicknames, typos, or any other reason. The ID number tells you these are all the same person, *while preserving the data in the name field as it was entered in the original records.*

Henrietta's case was an easy one. But as you sort through the records, you will inevitably come across contributors who may or may not be the same person. Here's an example:

| Name | Occupation | Zip | ContribID |
|------|-----------|-----|-----------|
| Wilson, Harold G | Buzzell & Jones | 60611 | WIL00393 |
| Wilson, Harold G Jr | Buzzell & Jones | 60611 | WIL00394 |
| Wilson, Harold G Sr | Retired | 60453 | WIL00395 |
| Wilson, Harry | | 60453 | WIL00396 |

How many Harold Wilsons have we got here? Two at least, since Jr. and Sr. are clearly marked. But what about Harold G or plain old Harry? You can't tell from the name alone, but you usually can tell from the address, occupation, or occasionally from other fields. The more fields you can view in context, the easier it will be. (That's why it makes sense to set up your computer screen in a row-and-column format. Squeeze as many columns as you can on your screen to make comparisons easier.) If you still can't tell who's who from the data you have, add a coded letter to the ID — an "X" would be appropriate — to indicate that this *may* be connected with another contributor, but you can't confirm it yet. In the case of the Messrs. Wilson above, you would handle the ID's this way:

| Name | Occupation | Zip | ContribID |
|------|-----------|-----|-----------|
| Wilson, Harold G | Buzzell & Jones | 60611 | WIL00393 |
| Wilson, Harold G Jr | Buzzell & Jones | 60611 | WIL00393 |
| Wilson, Harold G Sr | Retired | 60453 | WIL00395 |
| Wilson, Harry | | 60453 | WIL00395X |

Harold G. and Harold Jr. both have the same zip code and employer, so they're almost certainly identical. Harold Sr. lives in the same zip code as Harry, but you couldn't tell from this information alone whether he's the same as Harry Wilson. Only with the street address could you confirm it.

## STANDARDIZING EMPLOYERS AND OCCUPATIONS

Contributor names aren't the only fields in need of standardization. You'll also need to clean up the names of contributors' employers and occupations. When you start assigning category codes to each contribution, you'll use the contributors' occupations/employers to determine their financial interests. You'll also use the occupation/employer information to generate lists of the leading contributors — but to get accurate totals, you'll first have to standardize the employer names.

As with individuals, the best way to do this is to sort the employer field alphabetically. If the records you're working with have information on the contributors' occupation and employers, you'll want to *preserve that original data in the occupation and employer fields*. To do that, and to store the new standardized company names, you use a new field — newemploy. What goes in the newemploy field? If you know the contributor's employer *and* his or her occupation, enter the employer's name — duly standardized — in newemploy. If you have only the occupation *or* the employer, put whichever one you have in the newemploy field. And if you have no information at all about the contributor's occupation or employer, leave newemploy empty. Here's how it works:

| Name | Occupation | Employer | Newemploy |
|---|---|---|---|
| Cossett, Miles | | | |
| Wilson, Harry | Retired | | Retired |
| Farquard, Harold | Accountant | Farquard & Doe | Farquard & Doe |
| Barnwell, Linda | Accountant | Self | Accountant |
| Finley, Peter | Attorney | | Attorney |
| Obote, Milton | Lawyer | Smith & Jones | Smith & Jones |
| McAuley, Alex | Attorney | Smith and Jones | Smith & Jones |
| Chat, Felix | | Tasty Top | Tasty Top Bakery |
| Gateau, Bernard | Executive | Tasty Top Bakery | Tasty Top Bakery |

Once you've sorted the employer field alphabetically, do the same with the occupation field. As you do so, you will undoubtedly come across common occupations that don't line up alphabetically, but that are equivalent. Standardize those occupations under a consistent name in the newemploy field. Examples:

| | | |
|---|---|---|
| Attorney, Lawyer, Law | -> | Attorney |
| Physician, Doctor, Medical doctor | -> | Physician |
| Homemaker, Housewife, Domestic engineer | -> | Homemaker |

| | | |
|---|---|---|
| Real estate, RE, Real estate sales | -> | Real Estate |
| Insurance, Insurance agent | -> | Insurance Agent |
| Car dealer, auto dealer | -> | Car dealer |
| Educator, teacher | -> | Teacher |
| Accountant, CPA | -> | Accountant |

"Generic" occupations like these are not as critical as company names, since you won't be compiling them in your list of top contributors. They are handy, however, and there's nothing to be gained by having one total for "physicians," for example, and another for "doctors." On the other hand, don't sacrifice specificity for convenience. For example, don't convert "Real estate developer" into "Real estate" — or "Cardiologist" into "Physician." You might want to draw the distinction between each of those groups later, as particular legislative issues arise.

Once you've gone as far as you can in standardizing occupations/employers, and assigning IDs to each distinct contributor, it's time to standardize the newemploy field for each contributor with multiple IDs. One of the things you'll find as you go through the lists of contributions is that different candidates report different occupations for the same people. The more contributions a person makes, the more likely you are to turn up variations on what they do for a living. Here's an example:

| Name | Amount | Candidate | Occupation/Employer |
|---|---|---|---|
| Barnovski, Victor | $500 | Jones | Attorney |
| Barnovski, Victor | $250 | Fritz | Self-employed |
| Barnovski, Victor | $250 | Alexander | Barnovski & Schwartz |
| Barnovski, Victor | $500 | Eddington | Consultant |
| Barnovski, Victor | $250 | Montez | |
| Barnovski, Victor | $1,000 | Milton | Lawyer |
| Barnovski, Victor | $1,000 | Montoya | Barnovski & Schwartz |

If Mr. Barnovski had given only to candidate Montez, you'd never know what he did. Likewise with candidate Fritz. Fortunately, Barnovski spread enough money around that somebody finally got it right. From the information you can glean from all the reports, it appears that Barnovski is a partner in the law firm of Barnovski & Schwartz. This kind of variation in reported occupations/employers is commonplace — particularly among big givers who may in fact have several business interests. Often, the problem is not with the candidates, but with the lack of candor by people like Mr. Barnovski, who might have failed to fully identify himself (at least on paper) when giving his contribution. Be particularly wary of contributors from the Washington, D.C. area who list their occupation as "consultant." Many turn out to be lobbyists, but you won't be able to confirm that unless you consult a lobbyist directory, or find his name elsewhere in your database with a more accurate description of his livelihood.

# 11

# FINGERPRINTING CONTRIBUTORS

T he term "fingerprinting" contributors means expanding the information
you have on each contributor to include their occupation and employer, identifying other non-income-earning family members who
may have contributed, and checking to see whether they've made any ideologi-
cally-based contributions to a political action committee.

In states where the occupation/employer is not provided, the job of dis-
covering employers will be the most challenging step in the fingerprinting process. There are techniques to discover this information, and they'll be discussed
later in this section. Even if the occupation/employer is listed, there's still a bit
of work to do, as you'll uncover plenty of inconsistencies in the ways occupations are listed by different candidates.

The first step in the fingerprinting process, though, concentrates on finding other family members — spouses and children — who may have buttressed
the family breadwinner's contributions with gifts of their own.

## IDENTIFYING SPOUSES AND CHILDREN

The easiest way for a wealthy contributor to give more than the nominal contribution limit to the candidate of their choice is to give an extra contribution through their spouse. The number of contributors who do this is very large — so large, in fact, that the single biggest occupation listed on the rolls of the Federal Election Commission in a typical election cycle is "homemaker" or "housewife" or some similar variation.

Since most "homemakers" have no additional sources of income aside from their income-earning spouse, what you need to do is determine the family breadwinner's occupation/employer *and assign that same occupation to all other family members who don't have independent incomes.* In other words, if you identify William J. Harris as the president of First National Bank, and then you identify Rebecca Harris as his spouse, and Becky and Bill Jr. as his children, you assign the income earner's occupation/employer to all family members.

| Name | Employer | Newemploy |
|---|---|---|
| Harris, William J. | First National Bank | First National Bank |
| Harris, Rebecca | Homemaker | First National Bank |
| Harris, Becky | Student | First National Bank |
| Harris, William J. Jr. | Student | First National Bank |

Since you're doing this, you have to be sure when publishing the information, and compiling lists of top contributors, that you specify that your totals from each organization (in this case, First National Bank), include those of employees, officers *and* immediate family members. This is a legitimate way to account for the contributions, since it accurately tracks the economic interests of the contributors, but you have to be clear about your methodology.

The way to identify the spouses in the first place is to sort through the records so the husbands and wives (and any other family members) line up next to each other. The best way to do this is to sort by the last name, then by the zip code, like this:

| Name | Employer | Address | Zip |
|---|---|---|---|
| Harris, Pamela | Homemaker | 75 Cushman Place | 85011 |
| Harris, William J. | Accountant | 75 Cushman Place | 85011 |
| Harris, Joe | Retired | 88 Hazelnut St | 85023 |
| Harris, Loretta | Retired | 88 Hazelnut St | 85023 |
| Harris, Alexander | Consultant | 8381 Yucca Dr | 85023 |

By sorting the records in this way, most of the husband-wife combinations will be fairly obvious. Clearly, though, you're not going to match everyone this way. The most difficult case is when the two spouses list different addresses — the husband listing his office address and the wife listing the home address. Likewise, if the wife keeps her maiden name, she won't match up with her husband using this sorting method. One thing to watch for are hyphenated last names, an increasingly popular phenomenon on contribution rolls. If Juliet Wilson-Jones lists her occupation as homemaker, but her spouse doesn't turn up under W for Wilson, search J for Jones and you may find him.

You're never going to match every homemaker with his or her income-earning spouse, but you should be able to match the majority of them. If you've got a lot of "homemakers" left over with no apparent mates, sort the database again by the street address and try again.

However you match husbands and wives (and their children), once you've matched them, you've got to do two things: assign them the same contributor ID as the family breadwinner, plus an extra letter denoting that they're family members. At the Center, we add an A for spouse and B, C, D, E, F, etc. for children. So if the breadwinner's ID number is 39384, the spouse is 39384A, and their two "student" children are 39384B and 39384C.

Once you've copied the new ID number, you can also replicate the newemploy field of the family breadwinner. If it's First National Bank, copy that down to the spouse and all the children. Remember, this applies only to family members who do not have an independent income. If Frank Miller lists his occupation as attorney and Lynn Miller, his wife, lists hers as psychologist, don't change either one of their occupations. He gets coded as a lawyer; she gets coded as a psychologist. *You only copy down the breadwinner's occupation for members of the immediate family who do not have incomes of their own.*

## UNCOVERING OCCUPATIONS AND EMPLOYERS

It's one thing if your primary job is going through thousands of records standardizing occupations/employers and attaching them to spouses and children. It is quite another thing if your database covers a state where contributors don't report their occupations and employers and you've got to find them out on your own. In that case, you're going to need all the help you can get fingerprinting individual contributors. (You can use the same help if the contributor hasn't disclosed his occupation/employer despite state law.)

If you're dealing with major contributors — someone whose name keeps reappearing on multiple records — you might start by circulating the list of contributors to other reporters around the newsroom. Start with the political or statehouse reporters; they're the ones most likely to know if the giver is a lobbyist. It also helps to circulate "unknown contributor" lists to your news organization's remote bureaus around the state or region. Even if you don't recognize the name from your base in Chicago, the stringer in Peoria might very well recognize contributor names in that area.

If you're fortunate enough to be looking at an area that is covered by Polk or Johnson City Directories — those big, thick phonebook-like volumes with reverse address and phone listings — dig them out and start looking. Both Polk and Johnson City Directories include city residents' employers. To find out whether each of the directory publishers covers cities in your area, you can phone them. RL Polk & Co's customer service number is 804-353-0361. The Johnson Directories are no longer being published, but many libraries still have old copies.

Professionals are often listed in directories of their own, and the first one you should head to the library to dig up is the *Martindale-Hubbell Law Directory*. This multi-volume set is arranged by state and city, then alphabetically by lawyers and law firms. Considering the regularity with which lawyers contribute to political candidates (they gave $44 million to federal candidates in 1992), this is one book you might want to check your whole database against. Martindale-Hubbell also publishes a CD-ROM version of its directory — a far easier way to search for names than the hefty volumes, if you can find it at your library, or afford to buy a copy for the newsroom.

A similar professional volume, the *American Medical Directory*, lists all the nation's physicians. Published by the American Medical Association, it lists them alphabetically along with their city of residence. Your "hit rate" won't be nearly as good with this book as with Martindale-Hubbell, but it's an excellent reference if you're trying to determine whether "Dr. Milo Cohen" is a physician or a PhD.

Other obvious sources, if you've got the time, are plain old telephone directories — or new-fangled CD-ROM directories that cover white pages listings for the entire nation. Your best bet here is *PhoneDisc* (1-800-284-8353), which publishes four different CD-ROMs, ranging in price from $79 to $249 for more than 81 million residential phone listings and nine million businesses. It's not a complete directory — not only are unlisted numbers unlisted here, but neither are listings of people who withhold their home address. Nevertheless, the disks are an incredible bargain (they're widely available and heavily discounted). They're also a great way to track down old school chums you've lost track of over the years! Highly recommended.

## IDEOLOGICAL CONTRIBUTORS

It's dangerous to make assumptions about why people give money to politicians, and it's best not even to try. By using a person's employer as a means for coding their contribution you're making no assumptions at all — simply reporting on the contributor's source of income. But some contributors clearly give not because of their occupation or employer, but for ideological reasons. There is a way to identify these ideological contributors without inferring unknowable motives, but it involves an extra bit of work.

The way to identify ideological contributors is to examine the lists of contributions to ideological PACs. If Willie Johnson, for instance, gives $500 to the National Right-to-Life PAC, then gives $250 to a candidate who's supported by Right-to-Life, that contribution can rightly be categorized as Pro-Life, whatever Willie's occupation. The Center uses this technique when classifying contributions to federal candidates.

It is a very conservative approach, but it's one that can clearly be supported from the public record. In order to be classified as an ideological contribution, two elements must be satisfied:

- The contributor must have contributed to an ideological PAC, and
- The candidate must have received funds from an ideological group with the same interest.

If either criterion is missing, Willie's contribution will be based on his occupation. For example, if Willie Johnson gave another $200 to a candidate who received no money from pro-life groups, his contribution wouldn't be counted as ideological. Granted, these criteria are so conservative they undoubtedly undercount ideological contribution totals. But it's all you can say for sure based solely on the public record.

# 12

## CATEGORIZING CONTRIBUTIONS

The final stage of the fingerprinting process is the real payoff. In this phase of the research, you'll be assigning category codes to each contribution. The codes will correspond to the contributor's specific industry or interest group. When this phase is done, you'll have completed the database. All that will remain is reviewing it and finding whatever patterns stand out.

Though this is a rewarding step in the process, it's a challenging one. Now that you've determined that Winifred Wyzinski, for example, works for Wyzinski & Associates you've got to figure out what in the world Wyzinski & Associates does. Is it a lobbying firm? A trucking company? A management consulting firm? There's no telling from the name, so you'll have to find out elsewhere.

Fortunately, you can learn a surprising amount about what different companies do right on the shelves of your local library. Tens of thousands of corporations are listed and described — and their officers named — in publications such as *Standard & Poor's Register of Corporations, Directors and Executives* and Dun & Bradstreet's *Million Dollar Directory*. Doctors, lawyers, and many other professionals can be found in professional directories that you'll also find on the shelves of a well-stocked library. And if the companies are local, you can always phone them up.

The categorization process applies not only to individual contributors' employers. You'll be using the same categories for all classes of contributors — PACs, individuals, corporations and labor unions. For each one, you'll be trying to figure out which industry or interest group best describes what the contributor does, or what it stands for. Before reviewing the research materials that will help you categorize the contributors, an explanation of the categories themselves is in order.

The need for a system of categories is obvious, as soon as you start compiling contributions into a database. It is certainly useful to know who the biggest contributors are, and how much particular unions, companies and PACs are giving to political candidates. But what is even more important (and revealing) is figuring out how much whole industries are giving.

The Center's coding system had its roots in Alaska, where it was originally designed to match the patterns of political money going to members of the state legislature. That original system has undergone countless revisions over the years, along with a major expansion when the categories were applied to Congress. The system is still evolving; with each new election cycle we still tweak one or two categories, based on recent shifts in contribution patterns.

The coding system is hierarchical. At the very highest level, there are five super-categories: Business, Labor, Ideological/Single-Issue, Other and Unknown. Below that top level there are 13 "sectors," about 100 "industries" and in all, some 400 categories. A full list of all the categories is included in Appendix A, but for the moment, here's how the sectors and industries break down. (The most detailed "category" level has been omitted here to save space).

**Agriculture**
>Crop Production & Basic Processing
>Tobacco
>Dairy
>Poultry & Eggs
>Livestock
>Agricultural Services/Products
>Food Processing & Sales
>Forestry & Forest Products
>Miscellaneous Agriculture

**Communications & Electronics**
>Printing & Publishing
>Media/Entertainment
>Telephone Utilities
>Telecom Services & Equipment
>Electronics Manufacturing & Services
>Computer Equipment & Services

**Construction**
> General Contractors
> Home Builders
> Special Trade Contractors
> Construction Services
> Building Materials & Equipment

**Defense**
> Defense Aerospace
> Defense Electronics
> Miscellaneous Defense

**Energy & Natural Resources**
> Oil & Gas
> Mining
> Electric Utilities
> Environmental Services/Equipment
> Waste Management
> Fisheries & Wildlife
> Miscellaneous Energy

**Finance, Insurance & Real Estate**
> Commercial Banks
> Savings & Loans
> Credit Unions
> Finance/Credit Companies
> Securities & Investment
> Insurance
> Real Estate
> Accountants
> Miscellaneous Finance

**Health**
> Health Professionals
> Hospitals/Nursing Homes
> Health Services
> Pharmaceuticals/Health Products
> Miscellaneous Health

**Lawyers & Lobbyists**
> Lawyers/Law Firms
> Lobbyists/Public Relations

**Transportation**
> Air Transport
> Automotive
> Trucking
> Railroads
> Sea Transport
> Miscellaneous Transport

**Miscellaneous Business**
  Business Associations
  Food & Beverage
  Beer, Wine & Liquor
  Retail Sales
  Miscellaneous Services
  Business Services
  Recreation/Live Entertainment
  Casinos/Gambling
  Lodging/Tourism
  Chemical & Related Manufacturing
  Steel Production
  Misc Manufacturing & Distributing
  Textiles
  Miscellaneous Business

**Labor**
  Building Trade Unions
  Industrial Unions
  Transportation Unions
  Public Sector Unions
  Miscellaneous Unions

**Ideological/Single-Issue**
  Republican/Conservative
  Democratic/Liberal
  Leadership PACs
  Foreign & Defense Policy
  Pro-Israel
  Abortion Policy
  Gun Rights/Gun Control
  Women's Issues
  Human Rights
  Miscellaneous Issues

**Other**
  Non-Profit Institutions
  Civil Servants/Public Officials
  Education
  Retired
  Other

**Unknown**
  Homemakers/Non-income earners
  No Employer Listed or Found
  Generic Occupation/Category Unknown
  Engineers, unclassified
  Employer Listed/Category Unknown
  Unknown

Each category has its own five-character code, which is entered in the computer as the category is learned. The first character is a letter and generally corresponds to the sector — A for Agriculture, H for Health, etc. The other characters are numbers, which are also arranged hierarchically. As an example, Energy Production & Distribution is E1000, the Oil & Gas industry is E1100, Gasoline Service Stations are E1170.

Besides its own code, each category is also linked to higher "industry" and "sector" codes. So when you enter E1170 for Milo's Texaco, his contributions will be included under the Oil & Gas industry, and the Energy & Natural Resources sector.

### SIC CODES

The category codes for business types are based, loosely, on a system of business classifications developed by the U.S. Government's Office of Management and Budget. That system is known as the Standard Industrial Classification, or SIC code. The basic SIC code list is a set of four-digit numbers that covers virtually every conceivable type of business, from "abrasive products" to "yarn texturizing, throwing, twisting and winding mills."

The government uses these SIC codes to classify the millions of different businesses that operate in the U.S. More importantly, this standard government code has also been picked up by corporate directories, such as those put out by Standard & Poor's and Dun & Bradstreet. If you look up a company in *Standard & Poor's' Register of Corporations* (which you'll find in the business reference section of any moderately sized library), you'll find the name of the company, its top corporate officers, and a full listing of any SIC codes that describe the company's lines of business.

SIC codes based on Yellow Pages listings have also been used by a number of CD-ROM publishers to classify businesses. Look up Bank of America on the PhoneDisc Business CD-ROM, for instance, and you'll find it identified under the SIC code of 6021, National Commercial Banks — because that's the Yellow Pages category under which its ad was listed.

SIC codes are also used by several other invaluable CD-ROMs, including Dun's Business Locator, which uses the codes to identify over 9.2 million businesses across the country. (More on reference materials below.)

Electronic copies of the Center's category system are available from the Center for Responsive Politics at nominal cost. Phone the Center at 202-857-0044 for details.

It's possible that the Center's category system — which is designed primarily for congressional candidates, and is arranged to coincide with the jurisdictions of congressional committees — will need to be amended to fit your local circumstances. Feel free to amend it as needed, the system here is offered as a starting point. If you can keep fairly close to the coding system, however, it will help, if later you want to exchange databases with someone from another state, or to supplement the Center's coding of federal candidates with your own coding of state and local candidates.

## ASSIGNING CATEGORIES TO CONTRIBUTORS

There are any number of techniques for fingerprinting PACs, companies, labor unions, trade associations, and other contributors. For individuals, you'll be using the contributor's occupation/employer to determine the category code (unless you've identified them as an ideological contributor, as explained in the previous chapter).

It's often easiest to start with the PACs. First of all there are fewer of them, and they represent a large proportion of the campaign dollars at both the federal and state levels. At the federal level, PACs (or "political committees," as they're officially designated) don't have to declare to the Federal Election Commission what their agenda is. The only thing a PAC like "Citizens for Better Government" has to disclose is its name, address and treasurer. But if a PAC is sponsored by a corporation, labor union, trade association, or other organization, it must list its sponsoring group with the FEC.

The Realtors PAC, for example, is sponsored by the National Association of Realtors. If you're trying to categorize a state or local PAC that is affiliated with a federal PAC, your best bet may be to contact the Center and find out how we've coded it.

Most corporate and union PACs — even if your state doesn't have a counterpart to the FEC's "sponsor" — are relatively easy to identify simply from their name. The GTE Corporation Good Government Club represents GTE. The American Medical Association PAC represents the AMA. More problematic are ideological and single-issue groups, most of whose national PACs do not have sponsors. Americans for Good Government, for example, is a pro-Israel PAC, as is San Franciscans for Good Government and Citizens Concerned for the National Interest. Campaign America is a so-called "leadership" PAC sponsored by Senator Bob Dole of Kansas. Wish List is a PAC concerned with women's issues. The only way you're going to identify PACs with generic names like those is to ask them, or look them up if your state requires PACs to state their political agendas.

A good source for identifying federal PACs is the *Almanac of Federal PACs* by Edward Zuckerman (Amward Publishing). Updated biennially, it profiles all PACs that gave $50,000 or more to federal candidates and identifies their business or ideological interests.

Another good source is the Center's *Open Secrets: The Encyclopedia of Congressional Money & Politics.* The book identifies the primary interest of every PAC that gave $20,000 or more in the 1992 elections.

Before you can begin entering the codes, you've got to have a field in your database to hold them. If you haven't done it already, now is the time to add a five-character "catcode" field to hold the category code, and a second "source" field (10 characters or less in length) that you'll use to record how you identified the code.

| Data | Field name | Length | Field type |
|------|-----------|--------|-----------|
| Category code | Catcode | 5 | Character |
| Source | Source | 5 or 10 | Character |

For example, you look up Harold Farquard in the Martindale-Hubbell Law Directory and find that he's a lawyer for Smith, Farquard & Fritz of Seattle. Here's how you fill out the database:

| Name | Newemploy | Catcode | Source |
|------|-----------|---------|--------|
| Farquard, Harold | Smith, Farquard & Fritz | K1000 | MartHubb |

You can figure out many of the category codes simply by looking at the name of the contributor. If you see a contribution from the AT&T PAC, or from an employee or officer of AT&T, you simply look up the code for long distance telephone carrier — C4200. Since AT&T is a well-known company, and you know what business they're in, you can safely apply its code and put the source down as "Name." The same would be true of contributions from the American Medical Association, the National Rifle Association, or any other high-profile group.

Many other contributors can be identified by name even if you never heard of them before, simply because the type of business is evident from the name. Fred's Texaco is clearly a gas station, E1170. Betty's Beauty Salon is a beauty parlor, G5100. Mercy Hospital is a hospital, H2100. Gibson Pharmaceuticals makes drugs (H4300), Bandon Ford-Mercury sells cars (T2300), Main Street Savings & Loan is an S&L (F1200). Contributions from any of these can safely be categorized simply from the name.

When you're beginning the categorization process, a useful way to proceed is to search for certain key words in the "newemploy" field (or in the "contributor name" field if you're reviewing corporate contributions). Isolate, for example, every contribution with the word "Hospital" — or better, "Hosp", since you'll find plenty of abbreviations in the reports. Once you've got all the "hosps" on your computer screen, you can eyeball the records, make sure they're all hospitals, then mark them with the appropriate code. *Never* let the computer do this step automatically. The search of "hosp" may also turn up entries like "Ray's Animal Hospital," which should be classified under veterinarians, or "Vanessa's Hospitality Service" which might require further investigation. For that reason, even when you use the computer to search key phrases, *always* review each name by hand, or you're asking for trouble. And then there are always the bedeviling exceptions of companies with misleading names — Rhode Island Hospital Trust, for example, which is not a hospital at all, but a commercial bank. If you're at all in doubt, don't fill in the code based on the name alone. You can always look up the company later.

To help you grind through the lists of companies in your database, here's a partial listing of keywords that can help you identify the type of business. Again, don't automatically assume these codes follow, but search the keywords and go through each list one by one.

| Keyword | Type of business | Code |
|---|---|---|
| Hosp | Hospital | H2100 |
| Real, RE, R E | Real estate | F4200 |
| Nursing | Nursing home | H2200 |
| Sav, S&L | Savings & loan | F1200 |
| National Bank | Commercial banks | F1100 |
| Natl Bank | Commercial banks | F1100 |
| Ford, Olds, Buick, etc | Car dealers | T2300 |
| Toyota, Honda, etc | Japanese import dealers | T2310 |
| Truck | Trucking company | T3100 |
| ISD, USD | Public school district | X3500 |

Some codes can be applied based on the name of the contributor. Melvin G. Hobbes, MD is a physician, H1100. Rodney Jones, Esq. is a lawyer, K1000. A handful of other initials attached to names can also tell you what the contributor does for a living. Here's a short list:

| Abbreviation | Occupation | Code |
|---|---|---|
| MD | Physician | H1100 |
| DDS | Dentist | H1400 |
| Esq | Attorney | K1000 |
| CLU | Life insurance agent | F3300 |
| OD | Physician (osteopath) | H1100 |
| DVM | Veterinarian | A4110 |
| CPA | Accountant | F5100 |
| The Hon. | Public official | X3100 |
| Rev | Clergy | X0000 |

By the way, do not assume that "Dr." before a contributor's name means they're a physician. Dr. Henry Kissinger is not, nor are most people with PhD's. On the other hand, if you've got a number of otherwise unidentified contributors who list themselves as "Dr" you might want to check their names against a directory of physicians.

Fortunately for journalists who are trying to get a handle on the financial affiliations of political contributors, there is no shortage of reference materials that describe the business interests of different companies. You'll find many invaluable reference books on the shelves of your local library — look in the business reference section. Below is a rundown of some of the most valuable reference sources for identifying companies and contributors. Most are updated annually.

*Standard & Poor's Register of Corporations, Directors & Executives.* The biggest (and most useful) book in this three-volume set is the nearly 3,000-page listing of over 55,000 corporations. The companies are arranged alphabetically, and each listing identifies the companies' SIC codes and chief lines of business, their top executives, and in many cases their board of directors. It also provides their address and phone number, and additional data like their annual sales and number of employees. Two other smaller volumes complete the set. One lists some 70,000 corporate executives, along with their business affiliations. The other holds a number of indexes (including a very handy listing of all the SIC codes). Probably the most useful indexes are the Cross-Reference and Ultimate Parent indexes. Both of these link subsidiaries and affiliates with their corporate parents. If there's one book you should seek out above all others at the local library for help in identifying companies, this is the one. One caution, though: for the most part, these are not small companies. Ed's Towing, Farley's Bar & Grill, or Jones & Associates won't be listed. (Neither will most law firms or other professional offices, since they tend not to be corporations.)

*Million Dollar Directory*, published by Dun & Bradstreet Information Services. The format here is similar to Standard & Poor's. Corporate profiles are not as complete, but there are more of them — about 160,000 of them in the 1993 edition. It's a good backup or supplement to the S&P guide.

*Ward's Business Directory of U.S. Private and Public Companies*, published by Gale Research. Another useful publication, with the same general format as the books above, but without names of corporate executives. The 1993 edition listed 135,000 companies.

*Directory of Leading Private Companies*, published by the National Register Publishing Co. This reference, similar in format to the ones above, lists only privately-held companies with annual sales of $10 million or more.

*American Medical Directory*, published by the American Medical Association. This book lists, or attempts to list, every physician in the U.S. The names are arranged alphabetically, and show each doctor's name and city.

*Martindale-Hubbell Law Directory*, is the closest thing you'll find to listing every lawyer and law firm in America. Entries in this multi-volume set are arranged by state, then city, then alphabetically by lawyer and law firm. If you can find (or buy) a copy, try to get your hands on Martindale-Hubbell's CD-ROM version of the directory, which is much easier to search than the printed version — at least if you're a fast typist. Whichever version you get, this directory is a real gold mine, since lawyers are one of the very biggest contributor groups, and they give heavily through individual contributions as opposed to PACs.

All the above directories list companies and individuals from across the nation. Your local library may also have a number of regional directories that can be quite valuable when you're looking at contributors to state and local campaigns.

Specialized volumes like the *Texas Oil & Gas Directory* and the *Hollywood Creative Directory* are extremely useful, if your database includes contributors from either of those areas or industries. Similar directories exist in every region of the country. The best thing to do is search the shelves of the biggest libraries in your area.

One geographically specialized volume is worthy of particular note, as its focus is Washington, D.C. and its subject matter includes some of the most influential contributors in the nation. *Washington Representatives*, published by Columbia Books, is the definitive guide to lobbyists in the nation's capital. It lists both individuals and law and lobbying firms, *as well as their clients*. It's also cross-indexed, so you can quickly find out who represents a particular company or organization in Washington. If you're trying to track down Washington lobbyists, this book is invaluable. Highly recommended.

The most efficient way to use these reference books, if you can't borrow a copy for the newsroom, is to head to the library with a printout of the companies you're trying to identify. Scope out the books in advance, and make sure your printout is sorted in the same order as the book.

## CD-ROMS

The real frontier in directory publishing won't be found on bookshelves any more, but on computer. Many of the biggest publishers — including Standard & Poor's, Dun & Bradstreet and Martindale-Hubbell — are issuing electronic versions of their directories (often with more information than the printed version) on CD-ROM. These electronic versions, while sometimes prohibitively expensive, are an excellent reason for your newsroom to invest in a CD-ROM player if you don't already have one.

If you're unfamiliar with the technology, here's a quick description. CD-ROM stands for "compact disk — read-only memory." Beneath that humdrum nomenclature, however, lies the biggest revolution in media since the invention of the personal computer. The computer companies are hyping it to the hilt. "Multimedia" is their more glamorous buzzword. Essentially, a CD-ROM is a flat circular disk that looks identical to a music CD (it is), but instead of containing music, it contains data. Amazing quantities of data. Six hundred megabytes, to be exact — thousands and thousands of pages of text. The most popular CD-ROMs these days (like the growing number of multimedia encyclopedias) pack that little disk not with words so much as graphics and sound. The most useful ones for investigative reporters are light on the multimedia, but heavy on data. Unfortunately, many are also very expensive. If your newsroom can't afford them, hunt them down at the library.

*Dun's Business Locator.* A very expensive CD-ROM ($2,395 per year), but the best single source anywhere for millions of smaller companies all around the country. The most recent editions list over 9.1 million businesses. If you're trying to categorize "Jones & Associates" of New Orleans is, this is the place to find out. One caveat, however: Dun's lists an inordinate amount of businesses as "management services." Whether it's due to their interview techniques or some other reason, companies that shouldn't be classified this way often are. Aside from that one quirk, however, this disk is likely to be the most valuable one you'll find anywhere for identifying literally millions of companies that are listed nowhere else.

*Standard & Poor's Corporations.* This electronic edition of the classic *Standard & Poor's Directory of Corporations, Directors and Executives*, contains much more information than the book alone, though the price ($4,900 per year) tends to keep it in the hands of serious investors only. Much of it is more of interest to investors than to investigative reporters, but among the valuable things it does include are sections for most companies that describe more completely their different lines of business. This is most important when you're dealing with PACs sponsored by big, diversified corporations that could have multiple political interests. The CD-ROM often shows how much of the companies' revenues come from which source of their business — how much General Electric gets, for example, from its aerospace operations as opposed to its home appliance or power generation divisions. You can also search corporate executives by name, but beware — the "hit rate" on random searches in this database is pretty low. The disk is much more valuable for identifying the business interests of mid-sized to large corporations. (A less expensive version, which will consist of only the same material that's in the written edition, is in the works.)

*Martindale-Hubbell Law Directory.* This is an electronic version of the multi-volume print edition that lists virtually every lawyer in the nation. ($995 for a one-year subscription). Type in the name and up pops the entry that identifies the attorney's law firm, address, and a host of other information, including where they went to law school and when they graduated. Use this reference as a confirmation that a particular contributor is a lawyer, but be aware that lawyers do switch firms from time to time. If Martindale-Hubbell lists them as working for one firm, while their contribution report lists them with another firm, go with the contribution report, as it will have the latest information. This CD-ROM is also valuable for searching names of companies that sound like they're law firms. A good bet here is to search for any unidentified company names that consist solely of names (Kirkland & Ellis, for example), that include the words "et al" (Reed, Smith et al), or that have an ampersand (&) in their title — though you'll want to eliminate firms that have "& Co" or "& Son," as they tend not to be law firms.

*PhoneDisc.* If you have ever stumbled through the stacks of a large library poring through their collection of out-of-town telephone directories, you will thank your lucky stars for this disk. Or rather, this collection of four different sets of disks — PhoneDisc Business, which applies SIC code classifications to nine million businesses based on the category they appear under in Yellow Pages ads; PhoneDisc Residential, which offers 80 million residential phone listings from the nation's White Pages directories, Phone Disk ComboPack, business and residential listings in one package; and PhoneDisc PowerFinder, which includes business and residential listings, by phone number, address, SIC code and name on five regional disks. List prices for the packages range from $79 to $249, though they're widely discounted at mail order computer houses. Not as complete or reliable as Dun's Business Locator (since it's based on the secondary source of Yellow Pages listings), but only a tiny fraction of the price. Essentially, it's the poor man's Standard & Poor's. It's got its limitations, but what a bargain! This disk alone is reason enough to invest in a CD-ROM player for the newsroom. Highly recommended.

*Street Atlas USA* by DeLorme Mapping. It's a stretch to include this under campaign finance research materials, but it's such an amazing resource no newsroom should be without it. This one disk contains street maps of virtually every city, town, hamlet, highway and byway in America. You can zoom in to the town of your choice not only by typing in its name, but by typing its five-digit zip code, or even the area code and local telephone exchange, as in 202-857. Nearly every street in the country — interstate to gravel road — is in here, and nearly all of them are named. Once you've zoomed in to a particular city or town, you can type in the name of a street and the program will highlight it. In cities medium-sized and up, you can even look up addresses, like the 900 block of S. Halsted Street in Chicago! The list price is $169, but it's commonly discounted to $99 or less.

## REAL-WORLD CATEGORIZATION PROBLEMS

Though it would be ideal to categorize every contribution to every politician, given the realities of the data you're dealing with, it's a practical impossibility. Even in states where filling out the occupation/employer of each contributor is required, not every candidate fills out every blank in every report. Even those that are filled out are not always possible to classify. "Self-employed," for example, tells you nothing about the contributor's source of income that you can translate into an industry or interest group category.

In the Center's research into the 1992 federal elections, we were able to categorize approximately 70 percent of the individual contributions with some meaningful category code. The ones that got away fell into five categories:

**Homemakers, students and other non-income earners.** These are the contributors who don't draw a salary and who haven't been linked either with an income-earning spouse or parent, or with a contribution to an ideological PAC.

**Generic occupation — impossible to assign category.** These are the ambiguous descriptions — "self-employed," "businessman," "entrepreneur," etc. Without more information, you can't tell how they earn their money.

**Engineers, type unknown.** This is a subset of the "generic occupation" problem. If someone says they're an engineer, they could work in any number of industries — from construction to oil & gas, manufacturing, electronics, even railroads.

**No employer listed or discovered.** These are the blanks. No occupation has been listed on the contribution reports, and you've been unable to find the occupation through other means.

**Employer listed/category unknown.** Even when a contributor lists his or her employer, you're not always going to be able to find out what that company does. D&E Enterprises could be anything. If you can't find them in a business directory, and they're not in the phone book (or you haven't got time to call), you're out of luck.

Given enough time and resources (and state laws that require contributors to list their occupations and employers) it should be possible to categorize 90 percent or more of all contributions. But in the real world of budgets and deadlines and multiple responsibilities, there is never enough time nor all the resources you'd like to have at hand. You should be able to identify virtually every political action committee, as well as the great majority of corporate contributors. The challenge here is the money that comes from individuals. If you can categorize 60 or 70 percent of that you'll still be doing a job you can be proud of.

# 13

# SEARCHING FOR PATTERNS

Once your database is finished — you've categorized as many contributions as you can, and you've assigned "unknown" codes to all the rest — you're ready to begin compiling what you've got and digging up the patterns that stand out in bold relief. Just because the database is done, these patterns won't necessarily be obvious. Through the process of osmosis, you'll no doubt have picked up some interesting nuggets — an unexpectedly large concentration of funds from companies you might not have suspected, major bundling operations to specific politicians, etc. But the overall patterns of dollars going to the state legislature, for example, still need to be fished out of the data. To pull the trends out — and to find material for the stories you'll do later — there are a number of steps you can take.

Calculate totals for every category. This is a logical first step, and one that is guaranteed to show you things you'd never have known without doing all the research. To calculate category totals all you do is sort the database by the category code and have the computer generate totals. Save these totals as a separate file. What you'll have is a list like this:

| A0000 | Agriculture | $8,000 |
| A1000 | Crop production & basic processing | $83,039 |
| A1100 | Cotton | $500 |
| A1200 | Sugar cane & sugar beets | $12,300 |
| A1400 | Vegetables, fruit and tree nuts | $41,925 |
| A1500 | Wheat, corn, soybeans and cash grain | $10,050 |
| A1600 | Other commodities (incl rice, peanuts, honey) | $6,839 |
| A1300 | Tobacco & Tobacco products | $65,850 |

The next step is to aggregate these totals by industry and sector. Each category code — A1000, A1100, etc. — has an industry code associated with it. In the Center's category database (outlined in Appendix A), this code is named "catorder" and it consists of one letter and two numbers. The industry called Crop Production & Basic Processing, for, example, is coded A01, and it includes not just A1000, but A1100, A1200, A1400, A1500 and A1600 as well. Note that it does *not* include A1300 — tobacco is classified as an industry in its own right. The A0000 code, which is a catchall category for agriculture-related contributors that you can't put anywhere else, carries a catorder of A11 (miscellaneous agriculture).

When you total up the list above, here's what you come up with:

| A01 | Crop production & basic processing | $154,653 |
| A02 | Tobacco & tobacco products | $65,850 |
| A11 | Miscellaneous agriculture | $8,000 |

Do the same for all your categories, and you'll have compiled totals for approximately 100 industry and interest groups. The overall patterns will begin falling in place now, but 100 categories is still too many to illustrate in a simple graph that will show you at a glance which are the top contributors. To do that, you'll generate totals for each of 12 main sectors — Agriculture, Construction, Health, Labor, etc.

Just as each category has an industry or "catorder" attached to it, so it also has a sector attached to it. All the categories shown in the sample above fall within the Agriculture sector. Look in the appendix to see the sectors for each category code and you'll see how they all fit into place.

When you've generated totals for each sector, you'll have a list like this (the totals here are from the 1992 federal elections):

Agriculture ............................................................ $24,892,124
Communications/Electronics ................................. $21,232,464
Construction ......................................................... $15,246,489
Defense ................................................................. $8,328,760
Energy & Natural Resources ................................. $21,341,235
Finance, Insurance & Real Estate .......................... $71,091,876

| | |
|---|---|
| Health | $31,710,239 |
| Lawyers & Lobbyists | $44,058,744 |
| Miscellaneous Business | $38,478,007 |
| Transportation | $18,989,690 |
| Labor | $43,299,597 |
| Ideological/Single-Issue | $29,331,914 |

This information is compact enough to turn into a chart. You can do this in any spreadsheet program on your computer, or in a stand-alone graphics program. DeltaGraph on the Macintosh is an outstanding program for creating charts and graphs — and your paper's graphics department probably already has a copy.

But don't wait for the final publication of your stories to create a set of charts. *Graphing the summary data is an excellent idea at this stage,* even though you're not ready yet to put together the final graphics for your story. Unless you possess extraordinary powers of symbolic intuition, rows and columns of numbers, commas and dollar signs are not as effective in communicating patterns as a simple bar chart. The numbers, after all, are only symbols that represent patterns in reality. The chart is a direct, visual representation of those patterns. It's much easier to grasp intuitively — an important consideration when you're poring through piles of data trying to figure out what's significant.

Here's how the sector totals above show up as a graph:

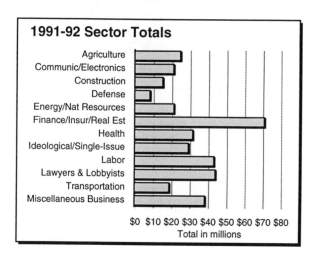

Even this simple graph is very revealing. We see immediately that the Finance/Insurance/Real Estate sector is the leading source of campaign funds, far ahead of any other sector. Labor and Lawyers head the second tier of top givers, and Defense stands out as the financial runt of the litter. But there's a lot more information you can also find out from the data you've already compiled.

Two of the most important elements that you can examine, and chart, are the breakdown between funds that came from PACs versus individuals (or PACs versus corporations, unions, and individuals, if your state allows all those groups to contribute), and the breakdown in contributions to Democrats and Republicans.

To get this information you'll have to go back to your original database and generate new totals. The first one is based on that single-character field that listed a code for the type of contribution — I for individual, P for PAC, etc. Sort the database by contribution type, then by category, and generate new category totals for PACs, individuals, etc. Aggregate the separate categories into industries and sectors, and generate a new chart. The chart below takes the same data we looked at above, and highlights how much came from PACs versus individuals in each sector.

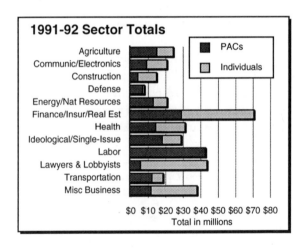

Immediately we have new insights. You can see, for example, that the great majority of contributions from lawyers and lobbyists comes from individual contributors, not PACs. The opposite is the case with labor donations — nearly all are delivered through political action committees. That's significant, it's worth a story, and it suggests a whole new line of questioning you can undertake when you begin doing interviews.

More revelations are in store when you break down the sector totals by party. To get to that point, though, you've first got to add a new field to the database — the party affiliation of each candidate. If you've already gathered this information and put it into a separate database of all candidates, it's a relatively easy matter to merge the two databases together and update your main database. All you need is a single field that's common to both databases, like a candidate ID. With most database programs, updating a field in one database with information from another is a relatively straightforward task.

When you've got the party information attached to each contribution, sort the database by party, then by category, and generate new totals. Graph them, again using the 1992 federal election data, and your new chart provides a whole set of insights:

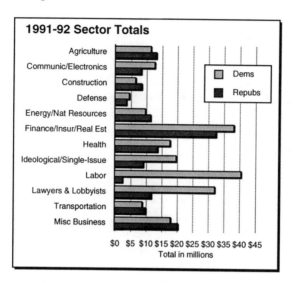

### 1991-92 Sector Totals

Agriculture
Communic/Electronics
Construction
Defense
Energy/Nat Resources
Finance/Insur/Real Est
Health
Ideological/Single-Issue
Labor
Lawyers & Lobbyists
Transportation
Misc Business

Dems
Repubs

$0 $5 $10 $15 $20 $25 $30 $35 $40 $45
Total in millions

The overwhelmingly Democratic tilt of labor unions now stands out dramatically. Lawyers and lobbyists also clearly favor Democrats by a wide margin, as do ideological and single-issue groups. Most of the other sectors split their dollars fairly evenly between the parties. The chart, and the numbers that go into it, once again suggest a whole new series of questions you'll want to pursue.

In fact, every chart you do, every summary total you generate, every way you look at the data — raises new questions and brings new insights. Some will be dramatic, others will be subtle. All bear further investigation. Looking at the data won't necessarily give you answers to all your questions, rather it will suggest the questions you ought to raise — of candidates, funders and political gurus alike.

Though the examples above deal with sector totals, you'll want to generate the same data, and many of the same exploratory charts, for every industry and category. Once you've generated totals at the category level, it's easy to aggregate the numbers into industries and sectors.

Here are some suggestions for other ways of looking through your database to find potentially interesting patterns:

*Calculate totals from business vs. labor vs. ideological/single-issue groups.* Labor is a sector by itself. So is Ideological/Single-Issue. Aggregate the ten business-related sectors (Agriculture to Miscellaneous Business) and you'll have the total for business contributors. When you total the numbers this way, you'll probably find the same pattern that's evident at the federal level — namely, that most contributions come from business groups. Unions and ideological groups may also be big contributors, but not when compared with the combined total of all business categories.

*Find out which industries are the biggest supporters of the Democrats and Republicans.* If you generate a list of the leading industries giving to candidates from each party, you will almost certainly find that some industries show up at or near the top of *both* parties' chief supporters. That means heavy political clout, no matter who wins at the polls — a red flag that ought to provoke a closer look at the industry's legislative agenda, and what it's received for its bipartisan investment.

*Calculate the industries that are most heavily partisan.* This is simply a percentage for each industry — what proportion went to Democrats versus Republicans. Labor unions, and a few ideological categories, will almost certainly top the most-partisan list for Democrats. But what other industries give heavily to them in your state? Likewise, which industries most strongly support Republican candidates?

*Calculate the fastest growing and fastest declining industries.* Obviously, this is one trend you won't be able to spot until you've got more than one election cycle to look at. But when you do, it will provide you with a very important bit of information. Most industries at the federal level are surprisingly consistent in their contributions from year to year. But if there's heavy political action on the horizon, look for an industry's contributions to soar. That's what happened to health care contributions in 1992, as Congress prepared to consider massive changes to the nation's health and insurance system. The National Rifle Association also greatly stepped up its giving in 1992 — a sign the NRA was trying to shore up its defenses against a rising tide of gun control legislation. If an industry — or an individual company or PAC — dramatically increases its giving from one election cycle to the next, you can be sure that something is afoot.

**III**

# REPORTING
# THE STORY

# 14

# REPORTING THE STORY

Once you've gathered the data and done the analysis, the possibilities for presenting what you've found in compelling stories are all but limitless. You have enough material in your database for *dozens* of stories. Some make sense to do right away, as soon as your research is finished; many others can follow weeks or even months later. Once you've got the database in order, you can mine it for stories for as long as you're covering politics.

When looking for story ideas, keep in mind the image of icebergs. Never assume that the money you've found is *all* the money, or the whole story. Assume that 90 percent of what's really going on is still beneath the surface. Use the money as your political dowsing rod, an indicator of underground streams of influence that are not visible to the casual viewer. Find out who's giving large amounts of money — and who's receiving it — and dig for your stories there. Here are some other hints and ideas:

**Look for trends.** Sharp rises and falls in money from a particular contributor, industry or interest group are signs of unusual political action. Measure which industries increased their giving the most from one election cycle to the next. If a big contributor dropped off the map, check further and find out why. Maybe they've rethought their legislative strategy, or maybe they got what they were looking for and don't need to give again for awhile.

**Go backwards in time.** The most complete data you've got is not for the election that's still going on, but for the last one. Combine last year's contributions with the results of the last legislative session and you have a complete case study ready to be cracked open. Start with a bill that made it through the legislature and follow the money that was sprinkled around as the bill moved through the process.

**Read the obits.** Quite often money isn't used to pass legislation, it's used to *stop* legislation, or make sure it never even gets as far as a vote. Take a look backwards at issues that never emerged for a final vote, bills that got bottled up in committee or quashed procedurally. It's much easier — and often less expensive — to *block* legislation than to pass it. So don't ignore legislative "failures" when you're looking for votes to correlate with money. If one lawmaker effectively killed a key bill, follow the money he or she got from the interests that benefited most.

**Who's Buying the Legislature?** Identify the top 20 contributors you've found. Some, undoubtedly, will already be known as major political players. Almost certainly, though, you will find some names on the list that no one would have guessed. List them all — or go deeper to the Top 50 or the Top 100. Present mini-profiles on each one. Show who got their money.

**Who *Are* These Guys?** Profile the top contributors, or some of the leading contributors in different categories. Who are the political rainmakers, people whose names appear not on the reports of three or four candidates, but dozens? No doubt the top contributor list will include a handful of the most powerful lobbyists in the state. Profile these guys. The politicians all know who they are, but few voters do. Give them a higher profile than they're used to.

**Payback.** Check the big contributors and see what they got for their investment. What bills passed by the last legislature directly affected them? What role did the top recipients of their money play in the passage (or burial) of the top contributors' key legislation? On stories like this, be sure to bring in the expertise of your statehouse political reporters. Show them what you've uncovered and work together to isolate instances where money decided the outcome of specific bills.

**Out-of-State Money.** This is a natural. How much of the money raised by candidates in the last election came from out of state? Where did it come from? Which politicians got the most out-of-state money, and why? This is a great story and it's easy to do on the computer. You've already got the data in there, all you've got to do is total the amount from within your state versus everything else. (When doing this, make sure to get a separate count for contributions from givers who listed no state at all.) Another caveat: beware using this measurement for PAC contributions. The Realtor's PAC, to take one example, is headquartered in Chicago, but its members are found everywhere. Half the PAC money in the 1992 federal elections came from the Washington, D.C. metropolitan area, but those PACs represented industries and interest groups from every state in the union. For these reasons, it's more accurate to do the instate/out-of-state breakdown only for individual contributors, or at most for individuals, corporations and unions.

## ELECTION SEASON STORIES & REPORTS

While the stories above can be done at any time, the peak of public interest in election information is naturally right in the middle of the campaign season. It's more difficult to do full-blown database analysis in the final weeks of an election, since all the contribution data isn't in yet, but you can still do computer-based stories on the money the candidates are raising. Here are some suggestions:

### Candidate Profiles

Side-by-side financial profiles of the candidates in each race. Highlight how much they've raised, plus whatever breakdown you can give of where the money came from. Ideally, this would include totals from each sector and a listing of the top industries giving to their campaign.

Realistically, this data won't be from the latest filing deadline, unless you are a super-fast typist and a Sherlock Holmes-class sleuth. Remember, though, the typical election cycle lasts two years, and many candidates (particularly incumbents) will have been raising money all along. The Center's final pre-election profiles of congressional candidates are based on reports filed with the FEC as of June 30. It's obviously not up-to-the-minute, but it's about as close as you're going to get to the final reports, if you're trying to analyze the details of each contribution.

You *can* use the latest reports as the basis for stories if you concentrate not on individual contributions, but on the summary data. You can certainly do rundowns of each candidate's total receipts and expenditures, plus whatever other data you can glean from the summary pages. In many states it's easy to do a breakdown of PAC vs. individual money, or PAC vs. corporate vs. union vs. individual money. And don't forget party money.

As part of your profiles, see if you can calculate what proportion of each candidate's contributions came from large vs. small contributors. You can do this quickly if the summary reports break down itemized vs. non-itemized contribution totals. If you've got more time, or the reports are small enough, you can even go through the itemized contribution reports page by page, totaling up all the large contributions and subtracting that number from the amount they list as their total receipts. You can set your own definition of what a "large" contribution is. A reasonable amount would be anything over $200 or $250 if it's a major campaign, or anything over $100 if it's a smaller one.

A little more time-consuming, but worth the effort, is a breakdown of in-state vs. out-of-state contributions. You can scan the reports quickly, looking just at the contribution amounts and the contributor's state. But keep in mind the caveats mentioned above — don't count PAC money and don't count contributions where no state is listed.

## Financial Competition

How many financially competitive races will voters face in this election? Do a district-by-district review of candidate spending and calculate how wide the spending gaps are. Congressional races are notoriously non-competitive financially. In each of the last three elections, the Center has found that in over half the congressional districts in the country, the winning candidate outspent the loser by a factor of *ten-to-one* or more! When the spending gulf is that dramatic, it's a fair question whether the voters are selecting the candidates on election day, or simply ratifying the choice made weeks and months earlier by the funding community. One candidate has the resources to introduce himself or herself to the voters, the other simply doesn't. How close are the spending figures in your state and local races? It's worth a look, and it's worth a story.

## POST-ELECTION STORIES

**How Many Financial Upsets?** In how many cases did the candidate who spent the most win? Be aware that on election day you're not going to have the final figures. Some reports won't come in until after the election. Still, you can go by what you've got as of the latest filings, and find out how many times the top-spender was successful at the polls. It's an easy, and natural, day-after story. There are several ways to easily expand this story — for example, you can compare open-seat races against those that featured incumbents versus challengers. You can also compare spending with vote percentages. Typically, the most expensive races are the ones most hotly contested.

**What Was the Price of Admission?** You'll have to wait for the final post-election or end-of-year reports to come in before you can do this story, which makes it a natural for the start of the legislative season. Simply tabulate the cost of each winning campaign and calculate the average cost of a seat in your state house, senate, city council, or whatever other legislative body you're tracking. It's simple to do, since all you need is summary figures, and it can be quite revealing. If your state senators serve for four or more years, be sure to add what they spent not just during the last two-year election cycle, but during the entire length of their term.

**Showdown at the Spending Gap.** At the federal level, the spending gap between incumbents and challengers is enormous — and it's growing with each new election cycle *(see the chart on page 33)*. See if you've got the same phenomenon in your state at the legislative level by calculating the averages in the last election.

### GRAPHICS

As every reporter these days knows, one of the fastest ways to an editor's heart is to pitch him a story with graphics. It's also the best way to let your readers (or viewers) absorb the data you've found without their eyes glazing over in a sea of numbers, commas and dollar signs. Campaign finance stories are among the easiest to illustrate with charts and graphs, since your database will allow you to generate them by the carload. When you do, there are a few considerations you need to keep in mind to make the graphics interesting, readable, and accurate. Here are some suggestions, and a cookbook of graphic ideas that can get you started.

### Race Comparisons

A very simple chart, yet one that is quite revealing, is a simple bar graph that shows how much the winner spent in every district versus the loser. The Center uses this graph in our *Price of Admission* book, the first book we do after each election. The chart is easy to put together, since it relies simply on summary data. Yet it often highlights what has become a very dramatic fact in congressional elections — that winners (overwhelmingly incumbents) typically spend vastly more on their campaigns than their challengers.

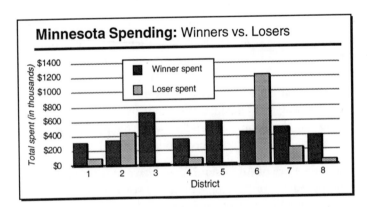

The race comparison charts also highlight the exceptional races — as in District 6 above — where the financial underdog was successful at the polls. (In the case above, the loser in District 6 was incumbent Democrat Gerry Sikorski. His vast advantage in funds didn't help him overcome the political fallout from bouncing hundreds of checks in the scandal-ridden House bank.)

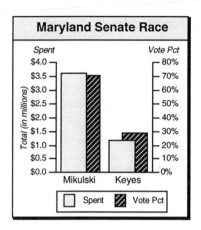

**Maryland Senate Race**

You can also do a one-on-one race comparison chart that contrasts each candidate's spending with the votes they received on election day. The Center uses these charts in *Price of Admission* to spotlight U.S. Senate races.

## Member Profiles

Candidate profiles — particularly profiles of candidates who were successfully elected — lend themselves particularly well to a variety of graphic treatments, both simple and elaborate. The Center's *Open Secrets* book, which features two-page campaign finance profiles of every member of Congress, includes the following graphic elements:

Three pie charts that summarize the member's source of funds, the breakdown in the PAC contributions by business vs. labor vs. ideological groups, and an easy-to-read chart that shows at a glance what proportion of their contributions from individuals came from out of state.

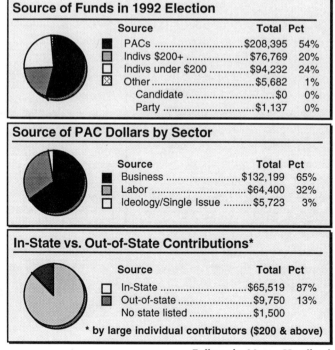

**Source of Funds in 1992 Election**

| | Source | Total | Pct |
|---|---|---|---|
| ■ | PACs | $208,395 | 54% |
| ▨ | Indivs $200+ | $76,769 | 20% |
| □ | Indivs under $200 | $94,232 | 24% |
| ⊠ | Other | $5,682 | 1% |
| | Candidate | $0 | 0% |
| | Party | $1,137 | 0% |

**Source of PAC Dollars by Sector**

| | Source | Total | Pct |
|---|---|---|---|
| ■ | Business | $132,199 | 65% |
| ▨ | Labor | $64,400 | 32% |
| □ | Ideology/Single Issue | $5,723 | 3% |

**In-State vs. Out-of-State Contributions***

| | Source | Total | Pct |
|---|---|---|---|
| □ | In-State | $65,519 | 87% |
| ▨ | Out-of-state | $9,750 | 13% |
| | No state listed | $1,500 | |

\* by large individual contributors ($200 & above)

The member profiles in *Open Secrets* include a full listing of the members' top contributors, arranged industry-by-industry, but it also includes this quick-reference chart that lets the reader see at a glance whether one contributor sector dominates. Notice the chart also shows the breakdown between contributions from PACs versus those from individuals.

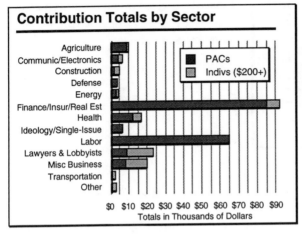

**Contribution Totals by Sector**

PACs
Indivs ($200+)

Agriculture
Communic/Electronics
Construction
Defense
Energy
Finance/Insur/Real Est
Health
Ideology/Single-Issue
Labor
Lawyers & Lobbyists
Misc Business
Transportation
Other

$0 $10 $20 $30 $40 $50 $60 $70 $80 $90
Totals in Thousands of Dollars

To give some perspective on the rising costs of campaigning, the *Open Secrets* profiles also include a graphic portrait of the costs of the member's last three election campaigns.

One of the most common phenomena in campaign spending is shown by the chart at right. Spending levels — particularly of incumbents — are most influenced by the presense (or lack) of a financially-credible opponent. In years when incumbents face woefully under-financed challengers, their own spending is fairly moderate. But introduce a challenger who can raise credible sums of money, and the spending by the incumbent goes through the roof. Those kinds of patterns jump out at you when you take the numbers from summary reports and turn them into graphs.

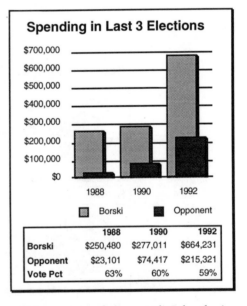

**Spending in Last 3 Elections**

$700,000
$600,000
$500,000
$400,000
$300,000
$200,000
$100,000
$0

1988 1990 1992

Borski    Opponent

|  | 1988 | 1990 | 1992 |
|---|---|---|---|
| Borski | $250,480 | $277,011 | $664,231 |
| Opponent | $23,101 | $74,417 | $215,321 |
| Vote Pct | 63% | 60% | 59% |

## Committee Profiles

One of the most interesting ways to document the influence of special interests is to track the money not member-by-member, but by committee. *Open Secrets* features two-page profiles of each committee in Congress, outlining the committee's jurisdiction, the top 20 contributors to committee members, and a chart that shows graphically which industries were the heaviest givers to members of the panel. The chart at right is that of the House Ways and Means Committee, the group that writes the nation's tax laws and, in 1994, one of the key committees dealing with health care reform. The graph shows clearly the flood of dollars from insurance companies, health professionals and lawyers — many of whom represented health and insurance clients.

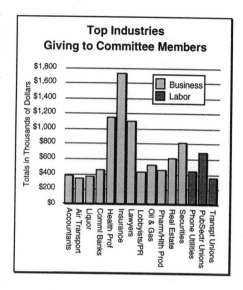

## Industry Profiles

Another fascinating way to look at the campaign finance numbers is to show how different industry groups distribute their dollars. While columns of numbers, like those in Section 1 of this handbook, tell the essential facts, they're no match for a chart, which can help readers absorb the patterns behind the numbers. Here's a chart showing the breakdown in contributions from the Energy & Natural Resources sector, broken down by party. Immediately, the reader can see not only that oil and gas companies were the biggest source of dollars in the sector, but that they had a decided preference for Republicans.

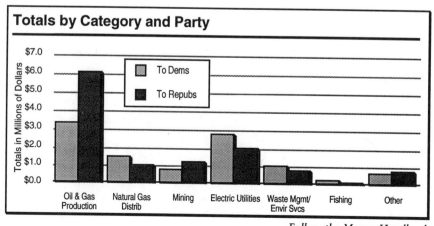

# IV

# APPENDICES

# APPENDIX A

## CATEGORY DESCRIPTIONS

The list of categories that follows is the system used by the Center for Responsive Politics in its coding of congressional and presidential contributions. Feel free to use is as a guide for setting up your own database, either adopted wholesale or modified as needed to fit your particular situation.

The first general rule about classifying contributions, whatever system you use, is to find the most specific category you can to fit the contribution. If nothing fits exactly, use the next most generic category. Most of the main sectors also include a "miscellaneous" category to hold contributions that don't fit elsewhere.

The second rule: if there's a conflict between the code of the employer and the code of the occupation, go with the employer. An accountant, for example, who works for Exxon, would be classified under oil & gas, not accounting. A lawyer who works for General Motors would go under auto manufacturing, not attorneys.

Be aware, too, that coding contributions is sometimes more an art form than a science. Sometimes it's not all that clear where to put a specific contribution. Use your best instincts, and if you're stumped, call the Center for advice at 202-857-0044. The Center can also supply you with a copy of this category database on disk.

# AGRICULTURE

## A01  Crop Production & Basic Processing

A1000  Crop production & basic processing
$1,748,430 contributed in 1991-92. PACs gave 6%.
This is the category for classifying farmers, if you don't know what kind of farmer they are, or if they're widely diversified.

    A1100  Cotton
    $453,751 contributed in 1991-92. PACs gave 78%.
    Cotton growers, cotton ginners.

    A1200  Sugar cane & sugar beets
    $1,801,818 contributed in 1991-92. PACs gave 83%.
    This category includes all sugar growers and sugar co-ops.

    A1400  Vegetables, fruits and tree nuts
    $1,188,860 contributed in 1991-92. PACs gave 60%.
    Vegetable and fruit growers are the biggest ones here. Note that in California, "ranches" often refer to fruit ranches, not cattle ranches as they do in Texas and other western states. So if you're looking at a "rancher" from California, don't automatically assume they raise only cattle.

    A1500  Wheat, corn, soybeans and cash grain
    $189,413 contributed in 1991-92. PACs gave 69%.
    Wheat, corn and soybeans are the big dollar crops in this category.

    A1600  Other commodities (including rice, peanuts, honey)
    $472,177 contributed in 1991-92. PACs gave 81%.
    Rice and peanut growers are the biggest ones in this category, but you can also use it for other crops that don't fit elsewhere.

## A02  Tobacco

A1300  Tobacco & tobacco products
$2,818,861 contributed in 1991-92. PACs gave 81%.
The biggest tobacco companies are widely diversified these days, but this is their primary category. It's also used for smaller tobacco farmers.

## A04  Dairy

A2000  Milk & dairy producers
$2,107,911 contributed in 1991-92. PACs gave 83%.
Dairy farmers and wholesale and retail milk, cheese and ice cream dealers. Dairy farmer cooperatives are the biggest source of money.

    A2300  Poultry & eggs
    $891,774 contributed in 1991-92. PACs gave 59%.
    Poultry growers and processors dominate this category.

## A06  Livestock

A3000  Livestock
$1,476,005 contributed in 1991-92. PACs gave 40%.
Cattle ranchers go here. (Note that "rancher" in California is sometimes used to describe fruit ranchers, not cattle ranchers.) In other states, you're safe to put "ranchers" here.

    A3100  Animal feed & health products
    $128,262 contributed in 1991-92. PACs gave 43%.
    Besides feed suppliers for farm animals, this also includes pet food manufacturers.

# AGRICULTURE *(CONT'D)*

A3200 Sheep and wool producers
$30,600 contributed in 1991-92. PACs gave 84%.

A3300 Feedlots & related livestock services
$153,900 contributed in 1991-92. PACs gave 79%.
Feedlots are the places cattle go to be fattened before they're slaughtered. The word "feedlot" is usually in the company name.

## A07  Agricultural Services/Products

A4000 Agricultural services & related industries
$625,743 contributed in 1991-92. PACs gave 79%.
A catchall code for diversified agricultural services companies, or ones you can't identify with any greater specificity.

A4100 Agricultural chemicals (fertilizers & pesticides)
$552,635 contributed in 1991-92. PACs gave 90%.
The biggest source of money within the agricultural services industry. It includes manufacturers as well as distributors. Since many of the biggest chemical manufacturers also produce agricultural chemicals, this is the best place to put such chemical companies when they're giving to lawmakers who sit on agriculture-related committees.

A4110 Veterinarians
$413,615 contributed in 1991-92. PACs gave 73%.
Note that veterinarians are classified under agriculture, not health care.

A4200 Farm machinery & equipment
$320,297 contributed in 1991-92. PACs gave 58%.
Dealers and manufacturers of tractors and other farm implements.

A4300 Grain traders & terminals
$462,575 contributed in 1991-92. PACs gave 64%.
This includes some very large companies (and contributors), such as Archer-Daniels-Midland.

A6000 Farm organizations & cooperatives
$604,564 contributed in 1991-92. PACs gave 99%.
This includes most farm co-ops (unless they're tied to a specific crop). Also organizations such as farm bureaus.

A8000 Florists & nursery services
$362,329 contributed in 1991-92. PACs gave 28%.

## A09  Food Processing & Sales

G2000 Food & beverage products and services
$582,289 contributed in 1991-92. PACs gave 66%.
Use this catchall category only for widely diversified companies that span two or more of the more specific categories below.

G2100 Food and kindred products manufacturing
$1,818,855 contributed in 1991-92. PACs gave 65%.
This includes companies that manufacture everything from baked beans to potato chips to frozen pizzas. This covers most of the food items you'd find in a local supermarket, except fresh produce and meat. Produce is classified under crop under fruits & vegetables (A1400). Meat processors are classified as G2300.

# AGRICULTURE (CONT'D)

G2300    **Meat processing & products**
$334,720 contributed in 1991-92. PACs gave 38%.
These are companies who make all varieties of meat products, including hot dogs, sausages, bacon, etc. These are companies that begin with meat from the stockyards and turn it into packaged products for supermarkets. Ranchers and other livestock and chicken producers are classified separately.

G2400    **Food stores**
$1,792,143 contributed in 1991-92. PACs gave 50%.
Retail food stores.

G2500    **Food wholesalers**
$580,057 contributed in 1991-92. PACs gave 53%.
These are wholesalers who supply retail food stores.

## A10  Forestry & Forest Products

A5000    **Forestry & forest products**
$1,253,349 contributed in 1991-92. PACs gave 43%.
This includes timber companies, sawmills, and others engaged in cutting down trees, but not retail lumber yards, which are classified as B5200.

A5200    **Paper & pulp mills and paper manufacturing**
$1,455,994 contributed in 1991-92. PACs gave 76%.
Paper & pulp mills go here. Manufacturers of paper packaging products — such as envelopes, paper bags, etc. — go under M7100.

## A11  Miscellaneous Agriculture

A0000    **Agriculture**
$257,597 contributed in 1991-92. PACs gave 0%.
This category is a catchall for all agricultural employers/occupations that can't be classified any more specifically. This is the code you give when the only occupation you have is, for example, "Agriculture" or "Agribusiness." It's also used when you have a company you can't identify, but whose name clearly identifies it as agriculture-related.

# COMMUNICATIONS & ELECTRONICS

## B00  Miscellaneous Communications/Electronics

C0000    **Communications & electronics**
$39,175 contributed in 1991-92. PACs gave 1%.
An umbrella category that's not often used for classifying contributors. Don't automatically put a company in here if they've got the word "Communications" in their name — they could be in public relations or some other field.

## B01  Printing & Publishing

C1000    **Printing, publishing & allied industries**
$515,330 contributed in 1991-92. PACs gave 0%.
Umbrella category. Use it only when you can't fit a contributor into one of the more specific categories below.

C1100    **Book, newspaper & periodical publishing**
$1,674,934 contributed in 1991-92. PACs gave 13%.
Includes newspapers, magazines and book publishers, and the people who work in those industries. "Journalists" go here, as do editors and writers.

# COMMUNICATIONS & ELECTRONICS *(CONT'D)*

> **C1300 Commercial printing & typesetting**
> $647,556 contributed in 1991-92. PACs gave 17%.

> **C1400 Greeting card publishing**
> $221,761 contributed in 1991-92. PACs gave 65%.
> An odd category, but one that merits its own listing primarily because of Hallmark and a couple of other firms that are fairly big contributors.

## B02 Media/Entertainment

**C2000 Entertainment industry/broadcasting & motion pictures**
$478,265 contributed in 1991-92. PACs gave 29%.
Use the C2000 code for widely diversified companies within the industry — such as Time Warner.

> **C2100 Commercial TV & radio stations**
> $1,075,656 contributed in 1991-92. PACs gave 46%.
> Use this for individual TV and radio stations as well as networks.

> **C2200 Cable & satellite TV production & distribution**
> $2,226,214 contributed in 1991-92. PACs gave 54%.
> This is the category for cable TV, as well as satellite TV services.

> **C2300 TV production & distribution**
> $570,666 contributed in 1991-92. PACs gave 16%.
> Independent TV producers go here, as do companies or individuals who specialize in video production or specific TV programs. TV actors and actresses go here as well.

> **C2400 Motion picture production & distribution**
> $2,596,760 contributed in 1991-92. PACs gave 13%.
> This is the category for the motion picture industry. It includes producers, directors, technicians, actors and actresses, and others involved in the industry such as agents. It does not include motion picture theater companies, which are classified under C2700.

> **C2600 Recorded music & music production**
> $591,482 contributed in 1991-92. PACs gave 40%.
> Recording artists go here, as do record companies, recording studios and anyone else involved in the recorded music industry. It does not, however, include musicians who play strictly in bars, clubs or other venues whose works are not recorded. They go under C2800.

> **C2700 Movie theaters**
> $62,060 contributed in 1991-92. PACs gave 0%.
> This only includes movie theaters. Others involved in the motion picture industry go under C2400.

> **C2800 Bands, orchestras & other live music production**
> $126,200 contributed in 1991-92. PACs gave 0%.
> Classify musicians here unless they also do recordings, in which case they go under C2600.

> **C2900 Live theater & other entertainment productions**
> $4,000 contributed in 1991-92. PACs gave 0%.
> Broadway, off-Broadway and off-off Broadway actors and actresses go here, as does everyone else in the live theater industry.

# COMMUNICATIONS & ELECTRONICS *(CONT'D)*

## B08  Telephone Utilities

**C4000  Telecommunications**
$110,447 contributed in 1991-92. PACs gave 7%.
An umbrella category. Use it only when you can't classify a contributor more specifically.

### C4100  Telephone utilities
$4,518,436 contributed in 1991-92. PACs gave 88%.
This is where to put local telephone companies, including the so-called "Baby Bells" like Bell Atlantic, NYNEX, Ameritech and US West.

### C4200  Long-distance telephone & telegraph service
$1,385,963 contributed in 1991-92. PACs gave 86%.
AT&T, MCI and Sprint go here, as do other companies that specialize in long-distance phone service.

## B09  Telecom Services & Equipment

**C4300  Cellular systems and equipment**
$187,195 contributed in 1991-92. PACs gave 39%.
Most cellular companies have the word "Cellular" in their names. Paging and beeper services also go here.

**C4400  Satellite communications**
$115,450 contributed in 1991-92. PACs gave 74%.
This includes all satellite communications companies, such as Comsat. Companies dealing exclusively in satellite TV go under C2200.

**C4500  Other communications services**
$14,200 contributed in 1991-92. PACs gave 58%.
A catchall category for telecom companies that don't fall into any of the other categories.

**C4600  Telephone & communications equipment**
$482,048 contributed in 1991-92. PACs gave 57%.
This includes companies that make telephones, switchboard equipment, walkie-talkies, etc.

## B11  Electronics Manufacturing & Services

**C5000  Electronics manufacturing & services**
$1,088,233 contributed in 1991-92. PACs gave 42%.
Use this category for most electronics firms, except those whose main work is defense related. Computer companies are classified separately.

## B12  Computer Equipment & Services

**C5100  Computer manufacturing & services**
$498,735 contributed in 1991-92. PACs gave 14%.
This category covers computer companies that are widely diversified, or that you can't identify with any greater specificity.

### C5110  Computers, components & accessories
$746,873 contributed in 1991-92. PACs gave 26%.
Manufacturers and dealers of computers, microchips, hard drives, monitors, or any other computer-related equipment.

### C5120  Computer software
$270,318 contributed in 1991-92. PACs gave 8%.
Software manufacturers and dealers. These are companies that specialize in off-the-shelf hardware. Those dealing with custom software or consulting go under C5130.

# COMMUNICATIONS & ELECTRONICS *(CONT'D)*

C5130  Data processing & computer services
$697,028 contributed in 1991-92. PACs gave 42%.
Computer consultants go here, as do others offering custom computer services.

# CONSTRUCTION

## C01  General Contractors

B0000  Construction & public works
$49,375 contributed in 1991-92. PACs gave 0%.
Umbrella category. Use it only when you can't be more specific.

B0500  Builders associations
$192,778 contributed in 1991-92. PACs gave 96%.
This is a specialized code that applies only to a few builders' groups that include both general contractors and residential builders.

B1000  Public works, industrial & commercial construction
$3,623,909 contributed in 1991-92. PACs gave 42%.
This is where general contractors go, as well as utility contractors, and companies that build commercial or industrial buildings, highways, or major public works projects.

B1500  Construction, unclassified
$2,634,132 contributed in 1991-92. PACs gave 0%.
If someone identifies themselves only as "Builder" and you don't know whether that covers commercial or residential construction, classify them here.

## C02  Home Builders

B2000  Residential construction
$2,017,905 contributed in 1991-92. PACs gave 59%.
Home builders go here, as do builders who specialize in apartments, condos or other residential construction.

B2400  Mobile home construction
$198,270 contributed in 1991-92. PACs gave 59%.
This includes only builders of mobile homes. Mobile home dealers and parks are classified under F4400. RV manufacturers and dealers go under T8200.

## C03  Special Trade Contractors

B3000  Special trade contractors
$580,886 contributed in 1991-92. PACs gave 12%.
This category covers subcontractors who can't be classified into one of the more detailed subcontractor categories below.

B3200  Electrical contractors
$436,146 contributed in 1991-92. PACs gave 37%.

B3400  Plumbing, heating & air conditioning
$513,447 contributed in 1991-92. PACs gave 33%.

B3600  Landscaping & excavation services
$155,949 contributed in 1991-92. PACs gave 0%.

# CONSTRUCTION *(CONT'D)*

## C04  Construction Services

**B4000  Engineering, architecture & construction mgmt services**
$1,327,535 contributed in 1991-92. PACs gave 45%.
Use this for construction and civil engineers, as well as companies that do both engineering and architectural work. Don't automatically put all contributors who identify themselves as "Engineer" here, though. There are engineers in virtually every field of business, from construction to manufacturing to oil & gas exploration. If you don't know what kind of engineer they are, put them into B4400.

### B4200  Architectural services
$574,357 contributed in 1991-92. PACs gave 6%.
This is the main category for architects and architectural firms.

### B4300  Surveying
$72,128 contributed in 1991-92. PACs gave 40%.
This includes construction and topographic surveyors, but not polling organizations, which go under G5200 or G5280.

## C05  Building Materials & Equipment

**B5000  Building materials**
$461,334 contributed in 1991-92. PACs gave 39%.
Use this broad code for dealers and manufacturers of building materials that are widely diversified — or ones who you can't identify more specifically.

### B5100  Stone, clay, glass & concrete products
$963,985 contributed in 1991-92. PACs gave 28%.
Sand & gravel companies (which often have the word "Aggregate" in their name) are among the firms that fit in this category.

### B5200  Lumber and wood products
$548,351 contributed in 1991-92. PACs gave 5%.
This is the category for lumber yards, but not for sawmills or other companies that chop down trees. (They go under A5000.)

### B5300  Plumbing & pipe products
$315,230 contributed in 1991-92. PACs gave 18%.
This includes all types of pipe products *except* those that specialize in oil pipelines. Those companies should go under E1150 (Oilfield service, equipment and exploration).

### B5400  Other construction-related products
$101,450 contributed in 1991-92. PACs gave 32%.
This would include companies that make or sell products — such as fences, elevators and flooring materials — that don't fall into any of the other building materials categories.

### B5500  Electrical supply
$160,922 contributed in 1991-92. PACs gave 0%.
Electrical supply dealers. These are usually easy to identify simply from their names.

**B6000  Construction equipment**
$318,400 contributed in 1991-92. PACs gave 30%.
This includes dealers and manufacturers of road graders, bulldozers, and other heavy construction equipment. Also crane rental companies.

# DEFENSE

## D01 Defense Aerospace

**D2000 Defense aerospace contractors**
$4,748,928 contributed in 1991-92. PACs gave 92%.
Many companies in this category also do civilian aerospace work. Put them here only if their main work is defense, or if they're giving to someone on a defense-related committee.

## D02 Defense Electronics

**D3000 Defense electronic contractors**
$2,433,503 contributed in 1991-92. PACs gave 86%.
Many companies in this category also do civilian electronics work. Put them here only if their main work is defense, or if they're giving to someone on a defense-related committee.

## D03 Miscellaneous Defense

**D0000 Defense**
$37,321 contributed in 1991-92. PACs gave 0%.
Defense is a sector that focuses most of its contributions at the congressional level, where decisions on defense spending are made. Many defense contractors are also actively involved in civilian work, and often you won't be able to tell if a company does defense work simply by looking at their SIC code. You'll have to dig deeper to find out whether they do defense work, and what proportion of their profits comes from that work. Government Executive magazine does publish an annual issue spotlighting the top 200 federal contractors, many of which are defense-related.

**D4000 Defense research & development**
$333,099 contributed in 1991-92. PACs gave 87%.
Often you can't tell from a company's SIC codes whether their work is defense-related or not. The publication listed above is a good source for identifying companies in this category.

**D5000 Defense shipbuilders**
$250,013 contributed in 1991-92. PACs gave 88%.
These are companies that specialize in naval shipbuilding.

**D6000 Defense nuclear contractors**
$11,200 contributed in 1991-92. PACs gave 0%.
A very specialized field that includes few contractors.

**D8000 Ground-based & other weapons systems**
$351,947 contributed in 1991-92. PACs gave 94%.
Companies that manufacture tanks, rifles, missiles, specialized military vehicles, etc. go under this category.

**D9000 Defense-related services**
$162,949 contributed in 1991-92. PACs gave 68%.
This includes everything from military commissaries to long-distance moving firms that specialize in moving military personnel and their dependents.

# ENERGY & NATURAL RESOURCES

## E01  Oil & Gas

**E1100  Oil & gas**
$1,645,123 contributed in 1991-92. PACs gave 22%.
Another umbrella category. If someone puts down "Oil industry," "Oil & Gas" or something similar, put them here.

**E1110  Major (multinational) oil & gas producers**
$2,699,335 contributed in 1991-92. PACs gave 84%.
These are the biggest U.S. producers — Exxon, Mobil, Texaco, etc. Smaller "independent" producers go under E1120.

**E1120  Independent oil & gas producers**
$2,048,958 contributed in 1991-92. PACs gave 26%.
They're called "independents" in the trade. These are the thousands of smaller oil companies that produce oil & gas or lease oil wells, or are otherwise involved in the production of oil.

**E1140  Natural Gas transmission & distribution**
$2,393,866 contributed in 1991-92. PACs gave 76%.
Natural gas pipeline companies go here. Their specialty is not producing natural gas, but transporting it around the country. Utilities that provide combined gas and electric service are classified under E1620.

**E1150  Oilfield service, equipment & exploration**
$1,039,863 contributed in 1991-92. PACs gave 43%.
This includes a wide variety of companies that support the oil industry, providing offshore or ground-based exploration services, oilfield equipment, and many other oil-related services in support of oil production companies.

**E1160  Petroleum refining & marketing**
$1,136,686 contributed in 1991-92. PACs gave 54%.
This is the category for companies that refine and market oil, but don't produce it. (All the big oil companies also do this, but their main business is producing the oil and they should be classified under E1110 or E1120.)

**E1170  Gasoline service stations**
$522,515 contributed in 1991-92. PACs gave 66%.
If you see a contribution from "Fred's Texaco" or other gas station owners, put it here. This is the retail end of the business, not the production of oil.

**E1180  Fuel oil dealers**
$78,047 contributed in 1991-92. PACs gave 5%.
These are local dealers who supply fuel oil.

**E1190  LPG/liquid propane dealers & producers**
$63,550 contributed in 1991-92. PACs gave 34%.

## E04  Mining

**E1200  Mining**
$119,210 contributed in 1991-92. PACs gave 34%.
Use this umbrella category when a contributor identifies themselves only as a "Miner" or "Mining engineer" or some other classification that makes it impossible to get more specific. Also use this for diversified mining companies.

**E1210  Coal mining**
$918,336 contributed in 1991-92. PACs gave 60%.
The biggest source of campaign dollars within the mining industry. Most of the dollars come from Kentucky and West Virginia.

E1220   Metal mining & processing
$685,217 contributed in 1991-92. PACs gave 70%.
This includes gold and silver mines and other types of metal mining and processing. Also includes aluminum smelting and processing.

E1230   Non-metallic mining
$89,334 contributed in 1991-92. PACs gave 55%.
Limestone, borax and other non-metallic mining operations go here.

E1240   Mining services & equipment
$32,663 contributed in 1991-92. PACs gave 8%.
Mining safety equipment manufacturers go here, as do others who provide equipment or services in support of the mining industry.

## E06  Nuclear Energy

E1300   Nuclear energy
$118,653 contributed in 1991-92. PACs gave 80%.
Most firms involved in nuclear energy — such as General Electric and Westinghouse — are also involved in other enterprises. Use this classification if their primary interest is nuclear energy, or if their contribution is going to someone on a committee that deals specifically with regulation of the nuclear energy industry.

E1320   Nuclear plant construction, equipment & services
$231,075 contributed in 1991-92. PACs gave 94%.
As with E1300, many of the companies who provide these services and equipment are also involved in other enterprises. Follow the same guidelines as E1300.

## E07  Miscellaneous Energy

E0000   Energy, natural resources and environment
$18,850 contributed in 1991-92. PACs gave 0%.
An umbrella category rarely used to classify specific contributors.

E1000   Energy production & distribution
$167,041 contributed in 1991-92. PACs gave 0%.
An umbrella category for energy-related companies. If they've got the word "Energy" or something similar in their name, but you can't classify them any further, put them here.

E1500   Alternate energy production & services
$32,250 contributed in 1991-92. PACs gave 49%.
This includes companies that deal with wind power, solar power, geothermal and any other types of alternative energy.

E1700   Power plant construction & equipment
$713,803 contributed in 1991-92. PACs gave 97%.
These are companies that build electrical power plants, or supply equipment or services for them.

## E08  Electric Utilities

E1600   Electric power utilities
$2,748,642 contributed in 1991-92. PACs gave 84%.
A major source of campaign funds on the national level. Note that utilities providing both gas and electric go under E1620 and rural electric co-ops go in E1610.

E1610   Rural electric cooperatives
$661,154 contributed in 1991-92. PACs gave 96%.
These utilities specialize in delivering electricity to rural areas. They almost always have the word "Co-op" in their company name.

E1620 Gas & electric utilities
$1,145,674 contributed in 1991-92. PACs gave 90%.
Use this for gas & electric utilities. Natural gas pipeline companies are classified under E1140.

## E09 Environmental Services & Equipment

E2000 Environmental services, equipment & consulting
$187,347 contributed in 1991-92. PACs gave 31%.
"Environmental engineers" go here, as do companies that specialize in environmental services and equipment.

## E10 Waste Management

E3000 Waste management
$1,529,834 contributed in 1991-92. PACs gave 55%.
This includes local refuse companies (many of which have the word "Carting" in their name). It also includes firms specializing in hazardous and nuclear waste.

## E11 Fisheries & Wildlife

E4000 Fisheries & wildlife
$700 contributed in 1991-92. PACs gave 0%.
An umbrella category that's rarely used in its own right.

## E12 Commercial Fishing

E4100 Fishing
$313,509 contributed in 1991-92. PACs gave 35%.
Commercial fishing operations are classified here, as are any sport fishing groups.

## E13 Hunting

E4200 Hunting & wildlife
$0 contributed in 1991-92. PACs gave 0%.
Commercial hunting guides would go here, as would organizations specifically dealing with hunting. Note that the primary legislative interest of many hunting groups really centers around gun owners' rights. Those organizations, like the National Rifle Association, are classified under J6200.


# FINANCE, INSURANCE & REAL ESTATE

## F03 Commercial Banks

F1000 Banks & lending institutions
$847,098 contributed in 1991-92. PACs gave 7%.
Use this when contributors identify themselves only as "Banker" or "Banking" or some other generic label that doesn't enable you to differentiate if they're a commercial banker or connected with an S&L. Check your local library shelves for banking directories that may help you connect the contributors with a specific banking institution.

F1100 Commercial banks & bank holding companies
$10,349,223 contributed in 1991-92. PACs gave 71%.
Commercial banks and their corporate parents go here. Note that any bank with the name "National Bank" or "State Bank" is commercial.

# FINANCE, INSURANCE & REAL ESTATE *(CONT'D)*

## F04   Savings & Loans

**F1200**   Savings banks and savings & loans
$1,318,827 contributed in 1991-92. PACs gave 70%.

## F05   Credit Unions

**F1300**   Credit unions
$697,305 contributed in 1991-92. PACs gave 95%.
Nearly all credit unions are easily identified since the words "Credit Union" almost always appear in their name. The abbreviation FCU also means Federal Credit Union.

## F06   Finance/Credit Companies

**F1400**   Credit agencies & finance companies
$1,042,551 contributed in 1991-92. PACs gave 55%.
Household Finance and similar loan companies go here. So do companies specializing in credit cards.

## F07   Securities & Investment

**F2000**   Securities, commodities & investment
$285,350 contributed in 1991-92. PACs gave 0%.
An umbrella category for the securities and investment industry. Use only if you can't classify a contributor any more specifically than this.

    **F2100**   Security brokers & investment companies
$10,383,262 contributed in 1991-92. PACs gave 17%.
Stockbrokers, brokerage houses, investment banking firms, bond dealers and similar investment industry contributors go here.

    **F2200**   Commodity brokers/dealers
$1,325,102 contributed in 1991-92. PACs gave 72%.
Commodities dealers and exchanges go in this category.

    **F2400**   Stock exchanges
$136,150 contributed in 1991-92. PACs gave 61%.
This is used for exchanges, such as the New York Stock Exchange or NASDAQ. Note that stockbrokers or brokerage houses, even those that identify themselves as members of the NYSE, are classified as F2100. Commodity exchanges go under F2200.

    **F2500**   Venture capital
$656,843 contributed in 1991-92. PACs gave 34%.
Many venture capital firms have the words "Venture Capital" in their names. This is their category.

## F09   Insurance

**F3000**   Insurance
$46,900 contributed in 1991-92. PACs gave 10%.
An umbrella category, rarely used for coding contributors. If you've got a diversified insurance company, or one you can't classify, put it under F3100.

    **F3100**   Insurance companies, brokers & agents
$9,109,055 contributed in 1991-92. PACs gave 54%.
Use this category for insurance companies or agents that are widely diversified. Also use this for contributors who identify their occupation only as "Insurance," "Insurance Agent," or something similar.

F3200 **Accident & health insurance**
$1,273,400 contributed in 1991-92. PACs gave 87%.
Among the companies that fall in this category are all the Blue Cross & Blue Shield affiliates, as well as all other health insurance companies. Note that "accident" insurance means accidents to individuals, not to cars. Auto insurance companies go under F3400.

F3300 **Life insurance**
$4,283,249 contributed in 1991-92. PACs gave 82%.
Use this for companies whose main line of business is life insurance. Also use this for contributors with "CLU" after their names. The abbreviation means "Certified Life Underwriter" and denotes a life insurance agent.

F3400 **Property & casualty insurance**
$232,174 contributed in 1991-92. PACs gave 73%.
Included in this category are companies that provide auto insurance, marine insurance and all other types of insurance that covers property as opposed to people.

## F10 Real Estate

F4000 **Real estate**
$1,937,926 contributed in 1991-92. PACs gave 0%.
Use this catchall code for contributors who identify their occupation only as "Real Estate" or "RE" or something similar. Otherwise, try to put them in one of the more detailed categories below.

F4100 **Real Estate developers & subdividers**
$3,797,455 contributed in 1991-92. PACs gave 8%.
Often these contributors will identify themselves only as "Developer." This is their category. You'll also find many home builders who do both — build houses and develop new subdivisions. Check their SIC code to see their main classification. (Builders usually go under construction. This category is more for investors and others who deal mainly with finances, not bricks and mortar.)

F4200 **Real estate agents & managers**
$7,626,300 contributed in 1991-92. PACs gave 40%.
This is where most of the real estate money comes from. Anyone who's a Realtor or real estate agent or broker goes in this category.

F4300 **Title insurance & title abstract offices**
$286,712 contributed in 1991-92. PACs gave 37%.
These companies almost always have the word "Title" or "Abstract" in their names.

F4400 **Mobile home dealers & parks**
$52,488 contributed in 1991-92. PACs gave 0%.
This is for mobile homes that people live in permanently, as opposed to RV's, which fall under T8200. It's also only for mobile home dealers and parks — not manufacturers. The manufacturers go under B2400.

F4500 **Building operators and managers**
$1,903,331 contributed in 1991-92. PACs gave 1%.
These are people or companies that manage residential, commercial and industrial properties (SIC codes 6512-6514). Also includes parking lots.

F4600 **Mortgage bankers and brokers**
$801,285 contributed in 1991-92. PACs gave 44%.
Mortgage companies of all types are classified here.

# FINANCE, INSURANCE & REAL ESTATE *(CONT'D)*

F4700   Other real estate services
$67,058 contributed in 1991-92. PACs gave 57%.
Among the specialties included in this category are real estate appraisers.

## F11  Accountants

F5100   Accountants
$4,877,052 contributed in 1991-92. PACs gave 51%.
Individuals and firms that provide accounting services. Contributors with "CPA" after
their names go here.

## F13  Miscellaneous Finance

F0000   Finance, insurance & real estate
$1,757,658 contributed in 1991-92. PACs gave 0%.
An umbrella category. Use this only if you can't classify a contributor with something more
specific. An example would be someone who classifies him or herself only as "Broker."
They could be a stockbroker or real estate broker, you can't tell which — so put them here.

F5000   Financial services & consulting
$157,046 contributed in 1991-92. PACs gave 5%.
A catchall category for contributors who can't be classified in any of the more specific
categories below.

    F5200   Credit reporting services & collection agencies
$142,915 contributed in 1991-92. PACs gave 43%.
These are companies that supply credit information on individuals to other
companies; also those that specialize in collecting debts. Loan companies and
credit card companies are classified under F1400.

    F5300   Tax return services
$42,475 contributed in 1991-92. PACs gave 47%.
Companies that help taxpayers file their tax returns are classified here.

    F5500   Other financial services
$342,440 contributed in 1991-92. PACs gave 42%.
Miscellaneous financial services that don't fit anywhere else.

F7000   Investors
$2,163,731 contributed in 1991-92. PACs gave 0%.
This is a "generic" category for contributors who identify themselves only as "Investor."

# HEALTH

## H01  Health Professionals

H1000   Health professionals
$40,946 contributed in 1991-92. PACs gave 1%.
Classify health professionals here only if you can't put them in one of the more specific
categories below.

    H1100   Physicians
$11,939,475 contributed in 1991-92. PACs gave 32%.
Put medical doctors here, unless they fit into one of the more specialized categories
below. Anyone with an "MD" after their name goes here. So do doctor
organizations, such as the American Medical Association.

        H1110   Psychiatrists & psychologists
$920,126 contributed in 1991-92. PACs gave 50%.

H1120   Optometrists & ophthalmologists
$1,719,077 contributed in 1991-92. PACs gave 78%.
These two groups often oppose each other legislatively, though they share a category. Ophthalmologists are medical doctors, optometrists are not.

H1130   Other physician specialists
$2,182,598 contributed in 1991-92. PACs gave 44%.
This is really an optional category. If someone identifies themselves as a "radiologist" or "cardiologist" or "pathologist," you can put them here, though the category is functionally equivalent to H1100.

H1400 Dentists
$2,281,306 contributed in 1991-92. PACs gave 70%.
Dentists go here. So do contributors who describe themselves as orthodontists or periodontists. A DDS after their name also means they're a dentist.

H1500 Chiropractors
$920,007 contributed in 1991-92. PACs gave 76%.
Chiropractors go here, not under H1100. They sometimes have the initials "DC" after their name.

H1700 Other non-physician health practitioners
$572,073 contributed in 1991-92. PACs gave 81%.
This includes nutritionists, audiologists and many other health professionals who are not physicians.

H1710   Nurses
$481,420 contributed in 1991-92. PACs gave 74%.
Nurses and nursing associations go here.

H1750 Pharmacists
$364,763 contributed in 1991-92. PACs gave 85%.
Note that drug stores, which sell a wide variety of products, are classified as G4900.

## H02   Hospitals/Nursing Homes

H2000   Health care institutions
$25,308 contributed in 1991-92. PACs gave 3%.
An umbrella category for hospitals and nursing homes.

H2100   Hospitals
$2,369,306 contributed in 1991-92. PACs gave 49%.

H2200   Nursing homes
$1,239,146 contributed in 1991-92. PACs gave 40%.
Nursing and convalescent homes go here, as do hospices.

## H03   Health Services

H3000   Health care services
$243,446 contributed in 1991-92. PACs gave 29%.
Umbrella category for a wide variety of health care services. Classify someone here only if you can't fit them in one of the other categories.

H3100   Home care services
$138,560 contributed in 1991-92. PACs gave 43%.
These are companies or individuals that specialize in the at-home treatment of medical patients. Many of these firms have "Home Care" in their name.

H3200   Outpatient health services (including drug & alcohol)
$194,015 contributed in 1991-92. PACs gave 11%.

    H3300  Optical services (glasses & contact lenses)
$19,850 contributed in 1991-92. PACs gave 22%.
Note that optometrists and ophthalmologists have their own category — H1120.
Use this category for opticians and for companies that sell (or make) glasses and
contact lenses.

    H3400  Medical laboratories
$68,412 contributed in 1991-92. PACs gave 7%.

    H3500  AIDS treatment & testing
$9,200 contributed in 1991-92. PACs gave 0%.

    H3700  HMOs
$448,789 contributed in 1991-92. PACs gave 41%.
Health maintenance organizations, commonly known as HMOs.

## H04  Pharmaceuticals/Health Products

H4000  Health care products
$191,060 contributed in 1991-92. PACs gave 51%.
Use this catchall category for highly diversified companies — like Johnson & Johnson —
that cover several of the more specific categories below.

    H4100  Medical supplies manufacturing & sales
$787,026 contributed in 1991-92. PACs gave 41%.
This category covers medical equipment manufacturers and dealers.

    H4200  Personal health care products
$157,100 contributed in 1991-92. PACs gave 78%.
The products in this category cover everything from Dr. Scholl's foot pads to
Band-Aids. It does not include pharmaceuticals, which are H4300.

    H4300  Pharmaceutical manufacturing
$3,147,717 contributed in 1991-92. PACs gave 76%.
This includes all varieties of over-the-counter and prescription drugs, from aspirin
to Prozac.

    H4400  Pharmaceutical wholesale
$156,468 contributed in 1991-92. PACs gave 33%.

## H05  Miscellaneous Health

H0000  Health, education & human resources
$1,088,045 contributed in 1991-92. PACs gave 0%.
An umbrella category. Not used for individual contributors unless their listed occupation
is so vague — "Health," for example — that they can't go anywhere else.

# LAWYERS & LOBBYISTS

## K01  Lawyers/Law Firms

K0000  **Attorneys & law firms**
$3,775 contributed in 1991-92. PACs gave 0%.
An umbrella category. The only contributors that would fall into this category are paralegals or legal secretaries.

K1000  **Attorneys & law firms**
$38,233,716 contributed in 1991-92. PACs gave 16%.
Use this category for attorneys and law firms, and for professional groups such as the American Trial Lawyers Association.

## K02  Lobbyists/PR

K2000  **Lobbyists & public relations**
$4,353,571 contributed in 1991-92. PACs gave 6%.
This category covers lobbyists and those public relations firms that concentrate on political issues or clients.

K2100  **Registered foreign agents**
$1,467,682 contributed in 1991-92. PACs gave 0%.
This category is specifically for lobbyists or others who represent foreign governments or clients and are officially registered as foreign agents with the federal government.

# TRANSPORTATION

## M01  Air Transport

T1000  **Air transport**
$117,954 contributed in 1991-92. PACs gave 8%.
Umbrella category. Try to use one of the more detailed categories below.

T1100  **Airlines**
$1,242,710 contributed in 1991-92. PACs gave 77%.
Scheduled and non-scheduled airlines, but not air freight, which goes in T1500.

T1200  **Aircraft manufacturers**
$423,090 contributed in 1991-92. PACs gave 81%.
This would include Boeing, Cessna, etc. Companies that make components for aircraft go in T1300.

T1300  **Aircraft parts & equipment**
$913,962 contributed in 1991-92. PACs gave 68%.
This includes most aerospace companies, except those whose primary business is defense-related.

T1400  **General aviation (private pilots)**
$491,356 contributed in 1991-92. PACs gave 98%.

T1500  **Air freight**
$51,000 contributed in 1991-92. PACs gave 45%.
UPS, Federal Express, and other express door-to-door delivery services go under T7100. All other air freight companies go here.

T1600  **Aviation services & airports**
$155,237 contributed in 1991-92. PACs gave 33%.

T1700  **Space vehicles & components**
$35,150 contributed in 1991-92. PACs gave 67%.
Some aerospace companies specialize in components for spacecraft or satellites. They go here.

# TRANSPORTATION (CONT'D)

T7100  Express delivery services
$2,224,752 contributed in 1991-92. PACs gave 99%.
This includes Federal Express and UPS, and other express delivery services that use air transport. For local courier and messenger services, use T7000.

## M02 Automotive

T2000  Automotive & trucking
$49,417 contributed in 1991-92. PACs gave 0%.
An umbrella category.

T2100  Auto manufacturers
$786,478 contributed in 1991-92. PACs gave 77%.
The Big 3 and any other automakers go in this category.

T2200  Truck/automotive parts & accessories
$840,264 contributed in 1991-92. PACs gave 44%.
This includes both manufacturers and dealers of auto parts and accessories.

T2300  Auto dealers, new & used
$3,211,769 contributed in 1991-92. PACs gave 56%.
If a contributor runs a car lot or car dealership, put them here, unless they specialize in Japanese imports, in which case they go into T2310.

    T2310  Auto dealers, Japanese imports
    $1,231,814 contributed in 1991-92. PACs gave 82%.

T2400  Auto repair
$76,294 contributed in 1991-92. PACs gave 4%.
Auto repair shops, tow truck services, etc.

T2500  Car & truck rental agencies
$298,468 contributed in 1991-92. PACs gave 29%.

## M03 Trucking

T3000  Trucking
$32,733 contributed in 1991-92. PACs gave 11%.
Umbrella category. Trucking companies go into T3100.

    T3100  Trucking companies & services
    $1,702,073 contributed in 1991-92. PACs gave 57%.
    These are long and short-haul trucking companies, and companies that support and supply them. Truck stops go under E1170, gas stations.

    T3200  Truck & trailer manufacturers
    $86,750 contributed in 1991-92. PACs gave 47%.

## M04 Railroads

T5000  Railroad transportation
$31,981 contributed in 1991-92. PACs gave 0%.
Umbrella category. Railroad companies go under T5100.

T5100  Railroads
$1,929,846 contributed in 1991-92. PACs gave 88%.
This is the category for railroads.

T5200  Manufacturers of railroad equipment
$146,915 contributed in 1991-92. PACs gave 27%.

# TRANSPORTATION *(CONT'D)*

T5300  Railroad services
$71,254 contributed in 1991-92. PACs gave 61%.
This includes switching services and rail yards.

## M05 Sea Transport

T6000  Sea transport
$188,130 contributed in 1991-92. PACs gave 1%.
Umbrella category. Only put contributors here if they do both sea transport and shipbuilding or repair.

T6100  Ship building & repair
$526,466 contributed in 1991-92. PACs gave 50%.

T6200  Sea freight & passenger services
$1,347,755 contributed in 1991-92. PACs gave 63%.
Cruise lines go here, as do barges and freight lines.

## M06 Miscellaneous Transport

T0000  Transportation
$127,646 contributed in 1991-92. PACs gave 0%.
An umbrella category that's rarely used unless the contributor simply identifies his/her occupation as "Transportation."

T4000  Buses & taxis
$57,725 contributed in 1991-92. PACs gave 23%.
Umbrella category. Only put a company here if they do offer both bus and taxi service.

T4100  Bus services
$207,305 contributed in 1991-92. PACs gave 51%.
Includes city transit systems and inter-city bus lines.

T4200  Taxicabs
$108,436 contributed in 1991-92. PACs gave 21%.

T7000  Freight & delivery services
$83,700 contributed in 1991-92. PACs gave 3%.
This category is mainly for local delivery services.

T8000  Recreational transport
$9,500 contributed in 1991-92. PACs gave 0%.
Umbrella category. Use the categories below to classify more specifically, if you can.

T8100  Motorcycles, snowmobiles & other motorized vehicle
$73,275 contributed in 1991-92. PACs gave 88%.
Also includes all-terrain vehicles (ATVs).

T8200  Motor homes & camper trailers
$24,851 contributed in 1991-92. PACs gave 0%.
These are Winnebagos and similar trailers and recreational vehicles, designed to be taken on the road. Larger mobile homes are classified under F4400 (mobile home dealers and parks) or B2400 (mobile home construction).

T8300  Pleasure boats
$61,200 contributed in 1991-92. PACs gave 77%.
Dealers and manufacturers of yachts, sailboats, cabin cruisers and motorboats go here, as do marinas. Big ships go under T6100 or T6200.

T8400  Bicycles & other non-motorized recreational transport
$22,434 contributed in 1991-92. PACs gave 99%.

# MISCELLANEOUS BUSINESS

## N00 Business Associations

**G0000  General commerce**
> $215,710 contributed in 1991-92. PACs gave 0%.
> Umbrella category. Not used to code specific contributors.

**G1000  General business associations**
> $92,254 contributed in 1991-92. PACs gave 94%.
> Includes a handful of national PACs that represent businesses of all types. Other than those few groups, this is not commonly used.

### G1100  Chambers of commerce
> $114,290 contributed in 1991-92. PACs gave 57%.
> Nearly all these groups — at the state, national and local level — have "Chamber of Commerce" in their name.

### G1200  Small business organizations
> $369,231 contributed in 1991-92. PACs gave 99%.
> Like G1000, this category is for a small number of national PACs that deal exclusively with the concerns of small businesses.

### G1300  Pro-business organizations
> $143,181 contributed in 1991-92. PACs gave 96%.
> Similar to G1000. Not commonly used.

## N01 Food & Beverage

NOTE: Food manufacturing companies are listed under the Agriculture sector.

**G2110  Artificial sweeteners and food additives**
> $14,700 contributed in 1991-92. PACs gave 24%.
> This is a small category for companies that specialize in sweeteners and other additives to food products.

**G2200  Confectionery processors & manufacturers**
> $111,490 contributed in 1991-92. PACs gave 20%.
> Candy manufacturers.

**G2350  Fish Processing**
> $168,410 contributed in 1991-92. PACs gave 13%.
> These are companies involved in the processing of fish products, not in catching or raising them. Commercial fishermen are classified as E4100.

**G2600  Beverages (non-alcoholic)**
> $388,539 contributed in 1991-92. PACs gave 70%.
> This category includes soft drinks, juices, and manufacturers of bottled water.

**G2700  Beverage bottling & distribution**
> $255,265 contributed in 1991-92. PACs gave 53%.
> These are the bottlers, not the manufacturers, of soft drinks. They're usually local or regional in their territory and are located all over the country. They almost always have the word "Bottling" in their company name.

**G2900  Restaurants & drinking establishments**
> $2,994,793 contributed in 1991-92. PACs gave 45%.
> Includes both restaurants and bars.

### G2910  Food catering & food services
> $130,840 contributed in 1991-92. PACs gave 35%.

# MISCELLANEOUS BUSINESS (CONT'D)

## N02 Beer, Wine & Liquor

**G2800** Alcohol
$6,400 contributed in 1991-92. PACs gave 0%.
An umbrella category for the more detailed classifications below.

**G2810** **Beer manufacturing**
$347,864 contributed in 1991-92. PACs gave 46%.
This includes breweries, but not wholesalers. Beer wholesalers (who provide most of the money from the beer industry) are classified under G2850.

**G2820** **Wine & distilled spirits manufacturing**
$1,356,172 contributed in 1991-92. PACs gave 59%.
This includes wineries and distilleries.

**G2840** **Liquor stores**
$95,627 contributed in 1991-92. PACs gave 1%.

**G2850** **Liquor wholesalers**
$2,273,554 contributed in 1991-92. PACs gave 52%.
The biggest money here comes from beer distributors, most of whom have the word "Distributing" in their company name.

## N03 Retail Sales

**G4000** Retail trade
$580,229 contributed in 1991-92. PACs gave 64%.
This umbrella category covers the retail industry as a whole. It's where you put shopping centers, or groups that represent the entire retail industry. If you're dealing with a retail store that doesn't fall into G4100-G4500, put it in G4600, miscellaneous retail stores.

**G4100** **Apparel & accessory stores**
$564,284 contributed in 1991-92. PACs gave 16%.
Clothing stores of all types go here, as do shoe stores.

**G4200** **Consumer electronics & computer stores**
$122,350 contributed in 1991-92. PACs gave 0%.
A small category, but usually easy to identify from the name of the company.

**G4300** **Department, variety & convenience stores**
$998,206 contributed in 1991-92. PACs gave 69%.
This includes department stores, five & dimes (if you can still find one these days), and convenience stores like 7-Elevens.

**G4400** **Furniture & appliance stores**
$284,881 contributed in 1991-92. PACs gave 0%.

**G4500** **Hardware & building materials stores**
$98,547 contributed in 1991-92. PACs gave 0%.
This is only for retail stores that sell hardware or a wide variety of building materials. Lumber yards go under B5200.

**G4600** **Miscellaneous retail stores**
$908,808 contributed in 1991-92. PACs gave 1%.
This covers everything that doesn't fit anywhere else in the retail category, from bookstores to jewelry stores to just about any other kind of specialty store you'd find in a shopping mall or downtown commercial district.

**G4700** **Catalog & mail order houses**
$225,963 contributed in 1991-92. PACs gave 42%.
These are companies that sell a variety of products through mail order or specialty catalogs.

# MISCELLANEOUS BUSINESS *(CONT'D)*

G4800 **Direct sales**
$209,979 contributed in 1991-92. PACs gave 24%.
Door-to-door and other direct sales operations, such as Amway.

G4850 **Vending machine sales & services**
$79,170 contributed in 1991-92. PACs gave 0%.
Most of these companies have the word "Vending" in their name.

G4900 **Drug stores**
$457,696 contributed in 1991-92. PACs gave 43%.
Drug stores carry just about everything these days, so they go here. Pharmacists, on the other hand, are classified under health care as H1750.

## N04 Miscellaneous Services

G5000 **Services**
$423,750 contributed in 1991-92. PACs gave 1%.
An umbrella category for personal services that don't fit in the categories below.

G5100 **Beauty & barber shops**
$75,363 contributed in 1991-92. PACs gave 0%.

G5300 **Equipment rental & leasing**
$324,813 contributed in 1991-92. PACs gave 50%.
These are companies that rent a wide variety of products. If they're specialized in one particular industry, classify them with that industry. Car rental agencies have their own code: T2500.

G5400 **Funeral services & cemeteries**
$306,098 contributed in 1991-92. PACs gave 21%.
This includes mortuaries, crematoriums and cemeteries.

G5500 **Laundries & dry cleaners**
$119,264 contributed in 1991-92. PACs gave 3%.

G5600 **Miscellaneous repair services**
$31,765 contributed in 1991-92. PACs gave 0%.

G5700 **Pest control**
$156,520 contributed in 1991-92. PACs gave 44%.
Put the local Orkin man here, but put crop dusters and other specifically agricultural pest control services under A4000.

G5800 **Physical fitness centers**
$84,190 contributed in 1991-92. PACs gave 0%.
These are spas, gyms, and other workout centers.

G6800 **Video tape rental**
$42,550 contributed in 1991-92. PACs gave 0%.
This is where to classify Blockbuster and other local video rental outlets.

## N05 Business Services

G5200 **Business services**
$2,520,185 contributed in 1991-92. PACs gave 3%.
Use this catchall category for any business services that can't be classified with any of the following codes.

G5210 **Advertising & public relations services**
$1,256,983 contributed in 1991-92. PACs gave 2%.
This includes advertising and PR companies — except those that specialize in political public relations, which are classified under K2000.

G5220   Direct mail advertising services
$198,916 contributed in 1991-92. PACs gave 58%.
This category also includes list brokers, who supply mailing lists to a wide variety of clients.

G5230   Outdoor advertising services
$644,017 contributed in 1991-92. PACs gave 37%.
Billboard companies go here.

G5240  Commercial photography, art & graphic design
$217,155 contributed in 1991-92. PACs gave 0%.

G5250  Employment agencies
$382,844 contributed in 1991-92. PACs gave 22%.
Also includes temp services.

G5270  Management consultants & services
$1,697,109 contributed in 1991-92. PACs gave 0%.

G5280  Marketing research services
$211,325 contributed in 1991-92. PACs gave 55%.

G5290  Security services
$374,126 contributed in 1991-92. PACs gave 34%.
This includes both rent-a-cop security services and companies providing burglar alarms and other security devices.

## N06 Recreation/Live Entertainment

G6000  Recreation/entertainment
$177,415 contributed in 1991-92. PACs gave 5%.
A catchall category that covers participatory and live entertainment and sports. The TV and motion picture industries have categories of their own in the Communications & Electronics sector.

G6100  Amusement/recreation centers
$421,013 contributed in 1991-92. PACs gave 21%.
This category includes everything from pinball arcades to bowling alleys and golf courses.

G6400  Professional sports, arenas & related equipment & services
$265,427 contributed in 1991-92. PACs gave 4%.
Professional sports teams and leagues go here, as do arenas for professional sports, such as Madison Square Garden.

G6700  Amusement parks
$28,650 contributed in 1991-92. PACs gave 0%.
These are local and regional parks, as opposed to internationally-known theme parks such as DisneyWorld which are major tourist destinations in their own right, and are classified as T9300 (resorts).

## N07 Casinos/Gambling

G6500  Casinos, racetracks & gambling
$740,605 contributed in 1991-92. PACs gave 31%.
Note that many contributions from Indian tribes are actually made because of gambling operations. If so, they belong here. (This is a fast-growing contributor segment — one worth keeping a close eye on.)

# MISCELLANEOUS BUSINESS *(CONT'D)*

## N08  Lodging/Tourism

**T9000  Lodging & tourism**
$76,350 contributed in 1991-92. PACs gave 26%.
Umbrella category. Use only when something doesn't fit into one of the more specific categories below.

### T9100  Hotels & motels
$1,014,488 contributed in 1991-92. PACs gave 29%.
Note that hotels in Las Vegas and other major gambling centers should be classified as casinos (G6500) if that's what they specialize in.

### T9300  Resorts
$127,933 contributed in 1991-92. PACs gave 14%.
These vary from remote fishing lodges to Disneyworld. The rule of thumb: if it calls itself a resort, or if it's a destination you'd travel a long distance to, classify it here.

### T9400  Travel agents
$376,368 contributed in 1991-92. PACs gave 18%.

## N12  Miscellaneous Business

**E5000  Water utilities**
$157,050 contributed in 1991-92. PACs gave 74%.
This includes water utilities that supply water primarily to urban and suburban customers. Irrigation districts and other water-related companies that specialize in delivering water to agricultural users are classified under A4000.

**G3000  Wholesale trade**
$344,191 contributed in 1991-92. PACs gave 33%.
Use this category only when the wholesaler deals with a wide variety of products. Beer and liquor wholesalers are classified under G2850. Wholesalers of specific products are classified in the closest category to that product.

**T7200  Warehousing**
$109,090 contributed in 1991-92. PACs gave 0%.

## N13  Chemical & Related Manufacturing

**M1000  Chemicals**
$2,184,662 contributed in 1991-92. PACs gave 57%.
Use this category for chemical manufacturers, unless they can be broken down into one of the more specific categories below.

### M1100  Explosives
$23,300 contributed in 1991-92. PACs gave 54%.

### M1300  Household cleansers & chemicals
$266,042 contributed in 1991-92. PACs gave 66%.

### M1500  Plastics & rubber processing & products
$528,022 contributed in 1991-92. PACs gave 12%.

### M1600  Paints, solvents and coatings
$74,393 contributed in 1991-92. PACs gave 20%.

### M1700  Adhesives & sealants
$12,200 contributed in 1991-92. PACs gave 20%.

# MISCELLANEOUS BUSINESS *(CONT'D)*

## N14  Steel Production

**M2100 Steel**
$870,603 contributed in 1991-92. PACs gave 32%.

## N15  Miscellaneous Manufacturing & Distributing

**M0000  Manufacturing**
$233,421 contributed in 1991-92. PACs gave 0%.
An umbrella category that is only used for a contributor if they identify themselves only as "Manufacturing" or something similar that can't be broken down further. Use the M-codes generally for manufacturers and distributors of the specific products mentioned.

**M1400  Manmade fibers**
$194,800 contributed in 1991-92. PACs gave 96%.

**M2000  Heavy industrial manufacturing**
$135,877 contributed in 1991-92. PACs gave 0%.
An umbrella category. Use it when the three categories below are not appropriate.

> **M2200  Smelting and non-petroleum refining**
> $76,440 contributed in 1991-92. PACs gave 0%.
> Aluminum smelting goes under E1220. All other smelting goes here.

> **M2300  Industrial/commercial equipment & materials**
> $1,651,109 contributed in 1991-92. PACs gave 29%.
> This is the catchall category for a wide variety of industrial and commercial equipment that doesn't fit anywhere else. This could include everything from sprockets to store fixtures.

> **M2400  Recycling of metal, paper, plastics, etc.**
> $220,346 contributed in 1991-92. PACs gave 26%.
> The biggest source of money in this category comes from scrap metal dealers.

**M3000  Personal products manufacturing**
$80,504 contributed in 1991-92. PACs gave 0%.
An umbrella category. Use this only if a contributor doesn't fit into one of the more specific categories below.

> **M3100  Clothing & accessories**
> $802,122 contributed in 1991-92. PACs gave 1%.

> **M3200  Shoes & leather products**
> $227,913 contributed in 1991-92. PACs gave 24%.

> **M3300  Toiletries & cosmetics**
> $344,012 contributed in 1991-92. PACs gave 16%.

> **M3400  Jewelry**
> $291,270 contributed in 1991-92. PACs gave 2%.
> This is for jewelry manufacturing and wholesaling. Retail jewelry stores go under G4600.

> **M3500  Toys**
> $63,659 contributed in 1991-92. PACs gave 0%.
> This is for toy manufacturing and wholesaling. Retail toy stores go under G4600.

> **M3600  Sporting goods sales & manufacturing**
> $73,015 contributed in 1991-92. PACs gave 4%.

**M4000  Household & office products**
$215,248 contributed in 1991-92. PACs gave 15%.
An umbrella category. If a contributor's business fits into one of the more detailed categories below, classify it there.

**M4100 Furniture & wood products**
$378,034 contributed in 1991-92. PACs gave 23%.

**M4200 Office machines**
$130,763 contributed in 1991-92. PACs gave 42%.
This includes Xerox machines, cash registers, etc., but not computers. Computer manufacturers and dealers are C5100 or C5110.

**M4300 Household appliances**
$158,950 contributed in 1991-92. PACs gave 54%.

**M5000 Fabricated metal products**
$540,047 contributed in 1991-92. PACs gave 8%.
This is a catchall category. Anything that's made of metal can go here, if there's no better place to put it.

**M5100 Hardware & tools**
$80,665 contributed in 1991-92. PACs gave 8%.
This is manufacturing and wholesaling only. Retail hardware stores are G4500.

**M5200 Electroplating, polishing & related services**
$58,225 contributed in 1991-92. PACs gave 7%.

**M5300 Small arms & ammunition**
$43,381 contributed in 1991-92. PACs gave 0%.

**M6000 Electrical lighting products**
$13,100 contributed in 1991-92. PACs gave 0%.

**M7000 Paper, glass & packaging materials**
$222,678 contributed in 1991-92. PACs gave 19%.
An umbrella category. Use this only if a contributor doesn't fit into one of the more specific categories below.

**M7100 Paper packaging materials**
$502,071 contributed in 1991-92. PACs gave 71%.
Use this code for companies that make cardboard, shopping bags, etc. Paper mills that turn wood into paper are A5200.

**M7200 Glass products**
$461,372 contributed in 1991-92. PACs gave 82%.

**M7300 Metal cans & containers**
$41,750 contributed in 1991-92. PACs gave 44%.

**M9000 Precision instruments**
$76,675 contributed in 1991-92. PACs gave 0%.

**M9100 Optical instruments & lenses**
$33,200 contributed in 1991-92. PACs gave 0%.

**M9200 Photographic equipment & supplies**
$22,450 contributed in 1991-92. PACs gave 0%.

**M9300 Clocks & watches**
$8,500 contributed in 1991-92. PACs gave 53%.

## N16 Textiles

**M8000 Textiles & fabrics**
$1,044,215 contributed in 1991-92. PACs gave 34%.
This is for textile mills. Manufacturers of manmade fibers go in M1400.

## LABOR

### P01  Building Trade Unions

**LB100  Building trades unions**
$6,904,679 contributed in 1991-92. PACs gave 99%.
Unions that represent construction-related workers, such as carpenters, plumbers, steel-workers, etc.

### P02  Industrial Unions

**LC100  Communications & hi-tech unions**
$1,426,390 contributed in 1991-92. PACs gave 100%.
This covers Communications Workers of America and similar unions involved in communications and hi-tech industries. Note that the IBEW has a separate category of its own (LC150).

**LC150  IBEW (Intl Brotherhood of Electrical Workers)**
$1,575,999 contributed in 1991-92. PACs gave 99%.
This category identifies members of the IBEW.

**LE100  Mining unions**
$459,600 contributed in 1991-92. PACs gave 100%.
The United Mine Workers is the primary union in this category.

**LE200  Energy-related unions (non-mining)**
$137,840 contributed in 1991-92. PACs gave 100%.

**LM100 Manufacturing unions**
$6,906,117 contributed in 1991-92. PACs gave 100%.
This includes unions that represent manufacturing workers.

### P03  Transportation Unions

**LT000  Transportation unions**
$1,750 contributed in 1991-92. PACs gave 0%.
An umbrella category only. All transport worker unions are categorized more specifically below.

    **LT100  Air transport unions**
    $1,657,643 contributed in 1991-92. PACs gave 100%.
    Includes unions representing aircraft pilots, flight attendants, mechanics, air traffic controllers, etc.

    **LT300  Teamsters union**
    $2,532,956 contributed in 1991-92. PACs gave 100%.
    Represents members of the Teamsters Union.

    **LT400  Railroad unions**
    $1,622,854 contributed in 1991-92. PACs gave 100%.

    **LT500  Merchant marine & longshoremen unions**
    $3,125,766 contributed in 1991-92. PACs gave 100%.

    **LT600  Other transportation unions**
    $1,275,700 contributed in 1991-92. PACs gave 100%.

### P04  Public Sector Unions

**L1000  Civil service & government unions**
$500 contributed in 1991-92. PACs gave 0%.
This is an umbrella category for public employee unions, each of which should be classified in one of the more specific categories below.

## LABOR *(CONT'D)*

L1100  Federal employees unions
$1,882,828 contributed in 1991-92. PACs gave 100%.
Unions representing federal government employees. Note that postal employees have their own category — L1500.

L1200  State & local government employee unions
$1,955,113 contributed in 1991-92. PACs gave 100%.
Unions representing government employees who work for state or local governments. Teachers unions are classified separately under L1300.

L1300  Teachers unions
$3,477,117 contributed in 1991-92. PACs gave 100%.
This covers teacher unions at all educational levels.

L1400  Police & firefighters unions & associations
$610,625 contributed in 1991-92. PACs gave 99%.
This category covers police and firefighters, whether in unions or other professional associations.

L1500  US Postal Service unions & associations
$3,822,198 contributed in 1991-92. PACs gave 100%.
This category is for postal workers, postal supervisors, postmasters, and all other groups or individuals that work for the US Postal Service. (Note that "USPS" stands for U.S. Postal Service, in case you see it on a contribution report.)

## P05  Miscellaneous Unions

L0000  Labor Unions
$869,240 contributed in 1991-92. PACs gave 96%.
This is an umbrella category that covers only organizations that cover all types of labor unions, such as the central AFL-CIO PAC. All other unions are classified in one of the more detailed categories.

L5000  Other unions
$164,063 contributed in 1991-92. PACs gave 100%.
Use this category for all labor unions that don't fit into any other more specific categories.

LA100  Agricultural labor unions
$1,940 contributed in 1991-92. PACs gave 48%.
Unions that represent agricultural workers.

LG000  General commercial unions
$1,250 contributed in 1991-92. PACs gave 0%.
Unions that represent commercial employees who don't fall into one of the more specific categories below.

LG100  Food service & related unions
$570,217 contributed in 1991-92. PACs gave 97%.

LG200  Retail trade unions
$1,518,786 contributed in 1991-92. PACs gave 100%.

LG300  Commercial service unions
$1,950 contributed in 1991-92. PACs gave 100%.

LG400  Entertainment unions
$31,750 contributed in 1991-92. PACs gave 100%.

LG500  Other commercial unions
$744,681 contributed in 1991-92. PACs gave 100%.

LH100  Health worker unions
$15,980 contributed in 1991-92. PACs gave 100%.

# IDEOLOGICAL/SINGLE-ISSUE

## Q01 Republican/Conservative

J1100   Conservative/Republican
$2,479,934 contributed in 1991-92. PACs gave 32%.
This covers a wide variety of PACs whose political agenda is broadly conservative, or who are associated with the Republican Party.

## Q02 Democratic/Liberal

J1200   Liberal/Democrat
$2,658,027 contributed in 1991-92. PACs gave 52%.
This covers a wide variety of PACs whose political agenda is broadly liberal/progressive, or who are associated with the Democratic Party.

## Q03 Leadership PACs

J2000   Leadership committees
$0 contributed in 1991-92. PACs gave 0%.
This umbrella category covers contributions from various "Leadership PACs," which are identified with a particular member of Congress or other political figure. Leadership PACs were given that name since they are traditionally used by incumbents to give money to other incumbents (or promising candidates) in the hope that the grateful recipients would then support their post-election campaign for a leadership position in the Congress.

   J2100   Democratic leadership PAC
$1,342,037 contributed in 1991-92. PACs gave 100%.
Leadership PACs associated with a Democratic member of Congress. In a state-level database, this could be used to apply to any Democratic member of the state legislature.

   J2200   Republican leadership PAC
$851,893 contributed in 1991-92. PACs gave 99%.
Leadership PACs associated with a Republican member of Congress. In a state-level database, this could be used to apply to any Republican member of the state legislature.

   J2300   Democratic officials, candidates & former members
$26,384 contributed in 1991-92. PACs gave 100%.
These are PACs associated with Democrats who are well known, but not a member of Congress (or a member of the state legislature in a state-level database).

   J2400   Republican officials, candidates & former members
$10,050 contributed in 1991-92. PACs gave 100%.
These are PACs associated with Republicans who are well known, but not a member of Congress (or a member of the state legislature in a state-level database).

## Q04 Foreign & Defense Policy

J5000   Foreign policy
$355,259 contributed in 1991-92. PACs gave 67%.
Use this umbrella category for PACs interested in foreign policy apart from the pro-Israel and anti-Castro issues that have categories of their own.

J5200   Anti-Castro
$159,000 contributed in 1991-92. PACs gave 100%.
PACs that support the eventual ouster of Cuba's Fidel Castro.

# IDEOLOGICAL/SINGLE-ISSUE *(CONT'D)*

JD100  **Defense policy, hawks**
$191,985 contributed in 1991-92. PACs gave 92%.
These are pro-military groups and groups that support a strong national defense.

JD200  **Defense policy, doves**
$370,918 contributed in 1991-92. PACs gave 53%.
These are groups that advocate non-military solutions to world crises and/or support a downsizing of the nation's military.

## Q05  Pro-Israel

J5100  **Pro-Israel**
$7,401,113 contributed in 1991-92. PACs gave 54%.
PACs that support stronger U.S. ties with Israel.

## Q06  Abortion policy

J7120  **Abortion policy, Pro-Life**
$486,407 contributed in 1991-92. PACs gave 85%.
Pro-Life and anti-abortion groups, such as Right-to-Life fall in this category.

J7150  **Abortion policy, Pro-Choice**
$1,317,768 contributed in 1991-92. PACs gave 65%.
These are pro-choice groups, which support a woman's right to obtain a legal abortion.

## Q07  Gun Rights/Gun Control

J6100  **Anti-Guns**
$169,512 contributed in 1991-92. PACs gave 95%.
This is for gun-control advocates, such as Handgun Control Inc.

J6200  **Pro-Guns**
$1,854,555 contributed in 1991-92. PACs gave 98%.
This category is for groups, such as the National Rifle Association, who are fighting gun control legislation and supporting the rights of Americans to own and bear arms.

## Q08  Women's Issues

J7400  **Women's issues**
$3,725,735 contributed in 1991-92. PACs gave 42%.
These are groups that support women's rights in general, and the election of more women to public office. Their political agendas often overlap the pro-choice groups (J7150), but generally include other issues as well.

## Q09  Human Rights

J7000  **Human rights**
$74,507 contributed in 1991-92. PACs gave 28%.
This catchall category can be used for any groups concerned with Human Rights that don't fall into one of the J7-series categories below.

J7300  **Gay & lesbian rights & issues**
$928,654 contributed in 1991-92. PACs gave 82%.
A growing segment of the contributor community, these are groups that support gay and lesbian rights.

# IDEOLOGICAL/SINGLE-ISSUE *(CONT'D)*

J7500    **Minority/ethnic groups**
$365,619 contributed in 1991-92. PACs gave 65%.
This category is for groups that support specific ethnic or minority groups. Note that many contributions from American Indian tribes are actually concerned primarily with legislation concerning gambling and casinos (G6500).

J7700    **Children's rights**
$453,800 contributed in 1991-92. PACs gave 100%.
KidsPAC goes here, as do all other groups specializing in child welfare.

JH100   **Health & welfare policy**
$512,855 contributed in 1991-92. PACs gave 29%.
Groups concerned with health and welfare policy in general, or with specific health care issues.

## Q10 Miscellaneous Issues

J1300    **Third-party committees**
$15,769 contributed in 1991-92. PACs gave 15%.
These are organizations connected with political parties other than the Democratic or Republican parties.

J3000    **Consumer groups**
$7,535 contributed in 1991-92. PACs gave 61%.
This category is for consumer-advocate groups.

J4000    **Fiscal & tax policy**
$111,404 contributed in 1991-92. PACs gave 86%.
This is for groups concerned primarily with tax policy or other government fiscal policies.

J7200    **Elderly issues/Social Security**
$1,167,425 contributed in 1991-92. PACs gave 100%.
These are groups dealing with senior citizen issues or the preservation of social security.

J7600    **Animal rights**
$24,850 contributed in 1991-92. PACs gave 21%.
Animal rights activists and organizations fall in this category.

J8000    **Labor, anti-union**
$374,006 contributed in 1991-92. PACs gave 92%.
These are groups that oppose organized labor and support state "right-to-work" laws.

J9000    **Other single-issue or ideological groups**
$209,944 contributed in 1991-92. PACs gave 64%.
Use this category for miscellaneous groups with specific issues that don't fall into any of the other ideological/single-issue categories.

JE300    **Environmental policy**
$1,633,398 contributed in 1991-92. PACs gave 73%.
Groups concerned with protecting the environment.

# OTHER

## W01 Other

**X0000  Other**
$662,357 contributed in 1991-92. PACs gave 9%.
A catchall category. Members of the clergy go here, as do any other contributors that just don't fit anywhere else.

**H6000  Welfare & social work**
$392,566 contributed in 1991-92. PACs gave 48%.
Social workers and agencies dealing with welfare issues go in this category.

**X5000  Military**
$125,803 contributed in 1991-92. PACs gave 0%.
This is the category for members of the armed forces or its civilian employees.

## W02 Non-Profit Institutions

**X4000  Non-profits**
$130,204 contributed in 1991-92. PACs gave 0%.
An umbrella category, and also a place to put non-profits that don't fit into any of the more specific categories below.

**X4100  Non-profit foundations**
$222,569 contributed in 1991-92. PACs gave 0%.

**X4200  Museums, art galleries, libraries, etc.**
$518,220 contributed in 1991-92. PACs gave 0%.
This includes public and private museums, galleries, etc., but not art galleries in the business of selling paintings; they go under G4600.

## W03 Civil Servants/Public Officials

**X3000  Civil servant/public employee**
$2,995,085 contributed in 1991-92. PACs gave 0%.
Use this category for public employees who don't fit into one of the categories below. This is the category for anyone who puts down the name of a city, state, county or other governmental organization, unless they're an elected or appointed official (in which case they go under X3100). Public employee unions go under Labor.

**X3100  Public official (elected or appointed)**
$152,295 contributed in 1991-92. PACs gave 0%.
Anyone with "The Hon" in front of their name goes here, as do legislators, mayors, governors, etc.

**X3200  Courts & justice system**
$345,231 contributed in 1991-92. PACs gave 0%.
This includes judges, prosecutors, prison officials, etc.

## W04 Education

**H5000  Education**
$585,559 contributed in 1991-92. PACs gave 0%.
Use this umbrella category to classify contributors who identify their occupation as "Educator" or "Teacher," without identifying their employer.

**H5100  Schools & colleges**
$2,355,025 contributed in 1991-92. PACs gave 0%.
This category applies to junior colleges and universities, and to private schools at any level. It does not include elementary and secondary level public school teachers and administrators; their code is X3500.

## OTHER (CONT'D)

H5150  Medical schools
$207,488 contributed in 1991-92. PACs gave 0%.

H5170  Law schools
$145,745 contributed in 1991-92. PACs gave 0%.

H5200  Technical, business and vocational schools & services
$373,522 contributed in 1991-92. PACs gave 34%.
Vocational schools have their own set of legislative priorities, distinct from those of other schools, hence their own category here.

X3500  Public school teachers, administrators & officials
$674,494 contributed in 1991-92. PACs gave 0%.
If you see the abbreviation "ISD" or "USD" that means independent or unified school district, and this is the category you put it in. People who work for private schools or academies go under H5000.

## W06 Retired

X1200  Retired
$15,930,210 contributed in 1991-92. PACs gave 0%.

# UNKNOWN

## Y00  Unknown

Y0000  Unknown
$85,426 contributed in 1991-92. PACs gave 100%.
An umbrella category. If it's a PAC and you haven't been able to identify its interest, put it here. If you're dealing with an individual contributor, classify it in one of the four categories below.

## Y01  Homemakers/Non-income earners

Y1000  Homemakers, students & other non-income earners
$13,650,755 contributed in 1991-92. PACs gave 0%.
If you haven't connected a homemaker, student, or other non-income earner with the family breadwinner, classify the contribution here.

## Y02  No Employer Listed or Found

Y2000  No employer listed or discovered
$33,504,033 contributed in 1991-92. PACs gave 0%.
Use this if they haven't filled out (and you haven't discovered) their employer. Also use this for federal contributions that list "Best Effort." All that means is that the campaign made an effort to find out the contributor's occupation, but weren't able to.

## Y03  Generic Occupation/Category Unknown

Y3000  Generic occupation - impossible to assign category
$3,021,287 contributed in 1991-92. PACs gave 0%.
This is for "Businessman," "Self-employed," "Entrepreneur" and other occupation descriptions that don't tell you anything about what they do for a living.

B4400  Engineers - type unknown
    $820,999 contributed in 1991-92. PACs gave 0%.
    This is where you put contributors who identify themselves only as "Engineer," unless you can tell what kind of engineer they are. Although this is a B-code, it's classified under the "Unknown" sector. Since there are so many different types of engineers, you can't tell which industry to stick them under without more information.

## Y04 Employer Listed/Category Unknown

Y4000  Employer listed but category unknown
    $33,592,383 contributed in 1991-92. PACs gave 0%.
    Use this when the contributor lists their employer, but you haven't been able to find out what type of business it is.

# APPENDIX B

# DOWNLOADING DATA
# FROM THE FEC

I f you want a stack of data to play with — a useful stack that your newsroom ought to have at its disposal anyway — sign up for the Federal Election Commission's on-line database. It costs $100 to set up an account with five hours of download time. Connect-time charges are $20 an hour, which is a bargain, considering all that you get for it. If you know what you're doing, here's what your investment will net you:

• Itemized lists of every contribution received by each U.S. House and Senate candidate in your state for the whole election cycle. This includes all contributions from PACs or political party committees, and every contribution of $200 or more from individual givers. Each contribution details the name, date, and amount of the contribution, plus the city and state (but not the street address) of the contributor. Contributions from individuals also include (or are supposed to include) the contributor's occupation/employer.

• Every contribution of $200 or more given by anyone who lives in your state to any federal candidate, PAC or national party committee. Again, you get the contributor's name, city and state, occupation/employer, and the list of whom they gave their money to.

• Every contribution from any PAC based in your state to any federal candidates or national party committee.

You can download all that information — in a format that can fit right into your own database — and still have plenty of money left over for the next election cycle, to go backwards in time to previous cycles, or to widen your inquiries to other states or candidates. For journalists, this is one of the best (and least publicized) bargains in Washington, and it's a gold mine for stories. Here's how to download from the FEC:

**Step 1.** Phone the FEC and tell them you want to set up an account on their Direct Access Program (DAP). Their toll-free number is 1-800-424-9530 (or 202-219-3730 in the Washington, D.C. area). You want the data systems department. They'll tell you to send in a check made out to "Ziff Information Services." Though you could send in as little as $20, that's only good for one hour of connect time. You're better off sending them $100 for five hours on-line. Send the check to the following address:

Federal Election Commission
Attn: Accounting Officer
999 E Street NW
Washington, DC 20463

**Step 2.** Wait. As soon as they get your check, they'll open an account for you and give you your own password. They'll also mail you a looseleaf binder filled with detailed steps for signing on and downloading different types of reports. The manual is useful, but its organization is sometimes confusing, as is its reliance on bureaucratic jargon. With the packet, you'll also get a list of local access numbers that allow you to hook up to the FEC without paying long-distance charges. Be sure to use a node that allows you to hook up at the fastest available speed — 9600 baud.

**Step 3.** Sign on, choose the reports you want and download the data to your own computer. Since you'll simply be looking at text, you need to set up your communications program to "capture" your on-line session and save it as a text file. If you don't know which report you want, or you want to explore, browse a while through the FEC's menu system. You can get detailed descriptions of each available report on-line. You can even set up your own files to store, for example, the ID numbers of every member of your state's delegation. That way, the next time you sign on, you don't have to enter the ID's one by one.

## DATA REPORTS VS. FORMATTED REPORTS

There are two ways to download data from the FEC, through "data" reports and formatted reports. Data reports consist of long strings of letters and numbers. They're designed to be split apart by your computer and entered as separate fields into your own database. Formatted reports are designed to be read directly on the screen or printed out. Here's an example of the difference between a data report and a formatted report:

*The formatted report:*

```
    H2OR01042    FURSE, ELIZABETH                          HOUSE
       OREGON                              DEMOCRATIC PARTY
INCUMBENT
          TOTAL RECEIPTS:                     603932
          TRANSFERS FROM AUTHORIZED COMMITTEES:      0
          INDIVIDUAL CONTRIBUTIONS:           351137
          NON-PARTY(E.G.PACS)OR OTHER COMMITTEES:  249751
          CANDIDATE CONTRIBUTION:                  0
          CANDIDATE LOANS:                         0
          OTHER LOANS:                             0

          TOTAL DISBURSEMENTS:                334820
          TRANSFERS TO AUTHORIZED COMMITTEES:      0
          INDIVIDUAL REFUNDS:                   1379
          NON-PARTY(E.G.PACS)OR OTHER REFUNDS:     0
          CANDIDATE LOAN REPAYMENTS:               0
          OTHER LOAN REPAYMENTS:                2000

                 BEGINNING CASH ON HAND:     7255
                 LATEST CASH ON HAND:      276367
                 DEBTS OWED BY:             12941

COMMITTEES INCLUDED:
     ELIZABETH FURSE FOR CONGRESS
               C00254169      THROUGH: 06/30/1994
```

*The data report:*

```
CNRH2OR01042FURSE, ELIZABETH                 HORDEMI      603932
0      351137    249751       0         0         0    334820
0        1379         0       0      2000      7255    276367
12941
```

If you just want a quick look at a candidate's latest summary filings, the formatted report is fine. But if you want to collect more detailed or lengthy data — for example, all the PAC or individual contributions to a member of Congress — you're not going to want hundreds of pages of computer printouts. Rather, you'll want the raw data so you can easily load it into your own database. In that case, the data report is the one you want to download.

In the looseleaf manual that comes with a subscription to the FEC's on-line service, you'll get a detailed breakdown of each of the fields in each report. The breakdown shows you how to break apart the strings of data into separate fields for your database. In the case above, for example, the first three characters show the record type, the next nine indicate the candidate ID, the next 38 characters show the candidate's name, etc.

Loading this into a database of your own is a simple matter. The process is described in detail below. But first, here's a rundown of the most useful reports you can download from the FEC.

### Candidate summary report.

This is called a 2S report if you'll be downloading it into your own database, or a 1S report if it's formatted. It gives you the latest summary numbers on any federal candidate. Included are the totals they've raised and spent, their current cash on hand, the totals they've received from PACs, individuals, and the candidate's own pocket. Download this report to get a quick comparison between competing candidates, or a whole state delegation. It's the one FEC report that is updated almost as quickly as the paper records come in. (The FEC estimates a 48-hour turnaround time from the time the report is received to when it's available on-line.)

### Individual contributions to candidates.

(Data report: 2I. Formatted report: 1I.) This report lists all contributions of $200 or more from individuals (as opposed to PACs or parties) given to a particular candidate or group of candidates. The data is taken directly from reports filed by the candidate. For each contribution, you get the following information:

*Name of the contributor.* This is stored in the FEC's computer as a single field — last name, followed by a comma, followed by the first name.

*City, state and zip of the contributor* — but *not* the street address. By law, FEC records cannot be used to solicit funds, so they leave off the street address to foil would-be abusers.

*Occupation/employer of the contributor.* You'll get one or the other, but not both. Sometimes you won't get anything. Most members of Congress provide some type of occupation/employer for the great majority — but not all — of their contributors. A few members fill in very little of this information. And you're going to find lots of things that aren't very useful — like "Businessman" or "Self-employed" or "Best Effort." (That last one means the campaign made its "best effort" to find out the occupation of the contributor, but hasn't turned up anything yet. Don't hold your breath.)

*Name and ID number of the candidate.* The FEC assigns a nine-digit ID to every federal candidate. This is useful. In your own database, you might want to substitute their official candidate names, however, with something more colloquial. Bill Clinton, for example, is stored in the FEC database as William Jefferson Clinton.

*Date of the contribution.* The FEC compiles the records by election cycle. When you request a type of report the first question you'll get will be which election cycle do you want to search — 1989-90, 91-92, 93-94, 95-96, etc. They usually keep the current and past two cycles available on-line.

*Amount of the contribution.* The lower limit is usually $200, though refunds are also included. The upper limit from individuals to candidates is $2,000 (you can give $1,000 for the primary and another $1,000 for the general election).

### Quarterly Data: PAC/Party Contributions to Candidates

(Data report: 4C. Formatted report: 3C.) This is the report you need if you want a full list of all PACs that have given to a particular candidate or set of candidates. The data report (4C) gives you an ID number for the PAC and the receiving candidate, the date and amount of each contribution, and a contribution code that tells you whether it was a regular contribution, an in-kind contribution, an independent expenditure, etc. To make sense of it, you'll also need to download the 6N report that lists all the PAC names that correspond to the ID numbers. The formatted report (3C) does list PAC names and sponsors, but it's hard to break down into a format that will fit into your database.

### PAC/Party Names, Addresses, etc.

(Data report: 6N.) This report, designed to be downloaded into your own database, gives you the name, sponsor, address and a host of other information about every "political committee" registered with the FEC. Since the FEC's definition of "political committee" refers not only to PACs, but also to candidate and party committees and a host of miscellaneous groups, you need to narrow your search before downloading this file. Here's how to do it:

When you say you want a 6N report, you'll see the following screen:

```
 ENTER 'A' TO SELECT BY COMMITTEE ID NUMBER OR WORD(S) IN THE COM-
MITTEE NAME
         'B' TO USE AN EXISTING COMMITTEE ID FILE
         'C' TO SELECT COMMITTEE(S) BY STATE, PARTY ETC.
         'X' TO RETURN TO THE MAIN MENU:
```

Type in "C." Next, this screen will come up on your computer:

```
YOU CAN SELECT COMMITTEES BASED ON SEVERAL CRITERIA,
   TO BEGIN THE SELECTION PROCESS:

ENTER '1' FOR ALL NON-PARTY (E.G.PACS) COMMITTEES
        '2' FOR ALL PARTY COMMITTEES
        '3' FOR ALL INDEPENDENT EXPENDITURE COMMITTEES
```

```
'4' FOR ALL COMMUNICATION COST COMMITTEES
'5' FOR ALL COMMITTEES
'6' TO SELECT COMMITTEES BY STATE
'7' TO SELECT NON-FEDERAL ACCOUNTS
'X' TO RETURN TO THE MAIN MENU

ENTER YOUR CHOICE NOW :
```

To get a list of all PACs (but not the thousands of other candidate, party and miscellaneous committees), type "1." In the jargon of the FEC, "non-party" committees equals PACs. Whatever you do, don't choose "5" or you'll get thousands of committees you don't really want.

### PAC/Party Contributions to Candidates

(Data report: 6C. Formatted report: 5C.) The name of this report makes it easy to confuse with the 4C/3C reports, but there's an important difference. This report gives you a list of contributions from a particular PAC or group of PACs. You pick the PAC and the report tells you which candidates got their money. With the 4C/3C report, you pick the candidate or candidates, and it tells you which PACs gave to their campaigns. This is the report you'd use if you wanted to download, say, all the contributions *given* by any federal PACs that operate from within your state. If you wanted a list of PAC contributions *received* by candidates in your state, you'd download the 4C or 3C report. There's one other important difference between the two reports. This report is updated each time the PAC files a new report. (Some PACs file monthly, others file quarterly). The 4C report is updated only once every quarter.

## INDIVIDUAL CONTRIBUTOR SEARCHES

Though it's not designated as a particular "report," the FEC also gives you the option of searching its entire database to find contributions by a specific individual or individuals. This is one of the most powerful and useful things you can get on-line. With it, you can search, for example, for all contributions to a candidate, PAC or party committee, from people whose last name is, say, "Keating."

You're not limited to just searching by names, either. You can search for all contributors who identified their employer as "Boeing," for example. Or anyone who listed their zip code as 20036. You can even search a *range* of zip codes. You can also search for all contributions from a particular state or city. And you can combine the search criteria, isolating, for example, all contributions that came from Texas during April 1994. You pick the criteria and seconds later, the FEC's computer will be churning out the list, straight to your computer.

If you choose to do some searches like this, there's one point you ought to keep in mind. If you're searching for contributors from a particular company, be aware that not all employees of that company are going to identify their employer completely or precisely with each contribution. In the Boeing search, for example, a particular contributor might list "Boeing" as their employer in one case, but only "Engineer" in another. Or the candidate they gave to might not put down anything at all in the employer field. *If you want a complete list of contributors from a particular company, the safest way to get it is to first search for the company name, then search all other instances of people with those names.* Clearly, this can be quite time consuming if the employer is a big one, but it's the only way to ensure your list is complete. If you're interested in a limited geographic area — say, all of Washington state, or the Pacific Northwest — it would probably be easier, and cheaper, just to download all contributors from those states, and do the searching on your desktop instead of on-line at $20 an hour.

## LOADING THE FEC DATA INTO YOUR OWN DATABASE

Once you've signed on to the FEC, captured the reports you wanted in a text file, and signed off again, you'll want to import the data into your own database so you can begin to play with it. Here's a quick guide on how to do it:

1) **Create the structure of your database.** You'll want a different database for each report. You can get the structure of the database by looking in the FEC's manual, as it lists all the fields for each different report. As an example, below is the FEC's description of the fields in the 2I report, Individual Contributions to Candidates. (When you download this report to a text file, each record will be exactly 135 characters long. This description tells you how to break apart this 135-character string into meaningful fields).

Committee ID                          Length 9                   Position 1-9
This is the ID number of the campaign committee receiving contributions.

Committee Type                     Length 1                   Position 10
     H = House campaign committee
     S = Senate
     P = Presidential

Committee Designation              Length 1                   Position 11
P = Principal campaign committee, the primary organization in the campaign.
A = Another committee authorized by the candidate to raise funds for the campaign.

Amendment Indicator                Length 1                   Position 12
Notes whether the contribution appeared on a new report (N) or an amendment to a report (A)

Report Type                              Length 3                  Position 13-15
A code that tells you which report the contribution was filed in — mid-year, post-election, etc.

Election Indicator                    Length 1                   Position 16
This is a one-letter code. "P" for primary, "G" for general election, etc.

| Transaction Code | Length 3 | Position 17-19 |
|---|---|---|

Code for the type of activity reported
15 = Cash contribution
15E = Cash contribution earmarked through another committee or individual
22Y = Contribution refund made to an individual

| Name of Contributor | Length 34 | Position 20-53 |
|---|---|---|
| Contributor City | Length 18 | Position 54-71 |
| Contributor State | Length 2 | Position 72-73 |
| Contributor Zip | Length 5 | Position 74-78 |
| Contributor Place of Business | Length 35 | Position 79-113 |
| Contribution Date | Length 6 | Position 114-119 |

Month, day, year - for example July 1, 1989 equals 070189

| Sign of Amount | Length 1 | Position 120 |
|---|---|---|

Refunds will have (-), contributions will have (+)

| Contribution Amount | Length 6 | Position 121-126 |
|---|---|---|
| Other ID | Length 9 | Position 127-135 |

In the case of an earmarked contribution, this will be the ID number of the party committee through whom the contribution was made.

Using the above list as your guide, create a database with one field for each of the fields shown above. All the fields — including zip codes — will be character fields, except the contribution amount, which will be numeric. You will need to invent shorter field names to fit in your database. The length of each field is the length shown above.

Once you've created the database, all you need to do is add one more field. Call this field "rawdata" and give it a length of 135 characters.

2. Open up the text file that you created during your on-line session and isolate just the part that has lists all the contributions for the 2I report. It will look something like this:

```
C00215905HPNQ1 P15 ASHRAF, NESIM              ROSEBURG
OR97470PHYSICIAN                   021694+001000
C00215905HPNMY P15 AVISON, WILLIAM J          LAKE OSWEGO
OR97035AVISON LUMBER COMPANY       050393+001000
C00215905HPN12PG15 AVISON, WILLIAM J          LAKE OSWEGO
OR97035AVISON LUMBER COMPANY       041394+000500
C00215905HPNQ2 G15 AVISON, WILLIAM J          LAKE DAWAGO
OR97035AVISON LUMBER COMPANY       041394+000500
C00215905HPNQ2 P15 BALDWIN, RICHARD F         EUGENE
OR97405SPRINGFIELD FOREST PRODUCTS 050294+000500
C00215905HPNYE P15 BEROIZHEIMER, MICHAEL G    STOCKTON
CA95267P & M CEDAR PRODUCTS        110593+000500
```

Save these records as a separate text file. Then close the file, go back to your database program and open up the empty database file you've created.

3. Import the records from the text file into your database file. You'll be importing all the records into the "rawdata" field.

4. Now you need to write a simple program in your database, a series of simple commands that tell the computer to break apart the string of characters in the "rawdata" field and distribute them into the other fields. The format will vary depending on the program you're using. Here's what it looks like in FoxPro:

```
replace all recipid with substr(rawdata,1,9)
replace all reciptype with substr(rawdata,10,1)
replace all recipdesig with substr(rawdata,11,1), etc.
```

When you've gone through and done this process once, you can simply save the list of commands in your database program and use them again the next time you're downloading a 2I report. The first time you do it takes a little work. The second time, you can download a file, load it into your database and begin playing with it, in less than 10 minutes. Contact your newsroom computer guru for help if you stumble along the way.

## NOW THAT I'VE GOT IT, WHAT DO I DO WITH IT?

Here are a few stories you can do just with the raw information:

• **Golden zip codes.** Where are most of the contributions coming from in your area? You can do totals on how much comes out of each zip code. You'd find an interesting map of average incomes if you translated the totals onto a map.

• **The top givers in your state.** Chances are few people knew these folks were out there. Who are they? Who are they giving to? Why are they giving all that money? Call them up. Is it ideological, or is it a pragmatic business investment? But before you do this story, you've got to search not just for individuals, but for organizations. Total up on the employer field.

• **In-state vs. out-of-state contributions.** How much are each of the candidates getting from out-of-state? (Remember, you're only looking at large contributions of $200 and over. But it's certainly worth looking at, particularly if one or two candidates are getting a lot of out-of-state money.)

Not only can you do a few relatively quick-and-dirty stories you otherwise would have missed, but you've got the makings of one dynamite database.

What newsroom *wouldn't* want to have a computerized list of all the big political contributors in their state? It's a great database to play with. Just troll through it and you'll find interesting things about politics in your own state that you never even knew before.

## CAVEATS

While the FEC's database is a valuable tool, it is not a panacea. There are a few important limitations to the data that you need to know about right from the start.

• First, while summary reports are entered into the computer within about 48 hours after they're received by the FEC, detailed reports listing each contribution suffer from what can be a considerable time delay. Despite the fact that virtually every congressional candidate, PAC and national party committee these days uses computers to manage their contribution reporting, the FEC is still not set up to receive data via modem or computer disk. Instead, they accept only paper records. *Reams* of paper records. The FEC then takes those records — most of which, ironically, are computer printouts — and hires inputters to type it again by hand into the FEC's computers. This would simply be silly (and a waste of taxpayers' money), if it were not for the unfortunate side-effect that *this delays posting of the data on the FEC's computers for several weeks and sometimes months.* During the last few weeks of the election season — just when interest in campaign finance data is at its highest — the FEC is typically five or six weeks behind in inputting the records. That means that the latest reports filed by candidates, PACs and parties won't be available until long after election day.

Ideally, the way to solve this problem (until the FEC solves it by accepting electronic filings), is to download everything you can get from the FEC, then enter the latest reports yourself from the candidates' paper reports. Another option worth considering is to use your clout as a news organization and go to the candidates directly, asking them for their contribution reports on disk. It's public information, after all, and you can always remind them that it's good politics to cooperate with the press. Obviously, this won't work if you're trying to cover the entire nation, but it could well prove fruitful if you're concentrating on just a handful of races.

• The FEC uses two different sources when entering contribution records into their computers. Contributions from individuals are taken from the reports filed by the candidates themselves. *Contributions from political action committees, however, are taken from reports filed by the PACs — not the candidates.* Inevitably, there are discrepancies between what the PACs report and what the candidates report. Usually, these are straightened out eventually —

but often only months after the election through a series of amended filings. Most of these discrepancies are fairly minor, but they can occasionally cause problems — particularly with candidates who have made a point of not accepting PAC contributions. For example, the XYZ PAC may report giving a $500 contribution to candidate Jones on October 6. Jones, who as a matter of principle, does not take PAC money, gets the check October 9 and returns it two days later. The refund won't be noted by the XYZ PAC until their next reporting period and meantime it will show up on the FEC's computer as $500 of PAC money to candidate Jones. Because of this, use extreme caution if you find PAC contributions on the FEC's computers to members who have foresworn taking PAC contributions. Always call the PAC or the candidate, or both, before writing any searing exposés labeling candidate Jones a mean-spirited hypocrite.

• The final caveat is one that is not unique to the FEC, but applies to any computer database: the data is only as accurate as the original records. Campaign treasurers often are volunteers, they are always working under deadline, and they themselves are working with records that may be incomplete and occasionally misleading. You'll find very few dollar errors in the FEC database (the FEC enters each record twice, then compares the two before accepting the entry), but minor variations in the spelling of contributors' names, their addresses and employers, are commonplace. That's why standardization of the computer records is an essential step when you're doing your own database.

## YET ANOTHER OPTION:
## THE CENTER FOR RESPONSIVE POLITICS

When you're dealing with federal records, you have another option available to you besides the FEC. The Center for Responsive Politics, which publishes this handbook, adds considerable information to the FEC's raw data. Specifically, the Center, a non-profit, non-partisan research group based in Washington, D.C., classifies each contribution to federal candidates and assigns it a category code.

The Center publishes numerous reports every year highlighting both the big picture and the details of congressional campaign finances. You can also call the Center at 202-857-0044, or the Center's National Library on Money & Politics (202-857-0318) to get customized computer-based reports on federal candidates. A partial list of Center publications appears on the next page in Appendix C.

# APPENDIX C

## RESOURCES FROM THE CENTER FOR RESPONSIVE POLITICS

The Center for Responsive Politics prepares a wide variety of publications every election cycle, detailing the patterns in money and politics at the national level. Among them:

### PACs in Profile

This is usually the first comprehensive report on federal campaign financing available after each election cycle. It reviews the big picture trends in PAC contributions, and is based on an analysis of the full two-year election cycle. This report is published in the spring after every general election. It's approximately 50 pages in length, and is free to news organizations.

### The Price of Admission

This is a district-by-district rundown of spending trends in the general election. Based on the summary reports filed by candidates, and preliminary analysis of PAC contributions, the book is over 200 pages in length and is usually published in late summer. The price is $20, but it's free to news organizations.

## Open Secrets

The flagship of the Center's publications, *Open Secrets* is a 1,300-page hardbound encyclopedia of congressional fundraising, published after each general election. It includes comprehensive two-page campaign finance profiles of every member of Congress, which include analysis of both PAC and individual contributions. It also features detailed profiles of the contributions flowing to each congressional committee, as well as profiles of each contributor sector and major industry, and statistical profiles of every PAC that gave $20,000 or more in contributions to candidates. Usually available about 18 months after the election, it is published by Congressional Quarterly Books. The third edition (covering the 1992 elections) costs $170.

## The Cash Constituents of Congress

A paperback distillation of *Open Secrets*, it includes the same information on committees, industries and big-picture trends, but only mini-profiles of each member of Congress. PAC profiles are limited to just those PACs that gave $50,000 or more. Also published by Congressional Quarterly Books, about one to two months after *Open Secrets*. The edition covering the 1992 elections costs $40.

## Soft Money

A comprehensive analysis of soft money contributions to the federal parties is published by the Center after every general election. This publication lists the top soft money contributors, along with an industry-by-industry breakdown of contributors to each political party. Generally available the summer after each general election. Free to the news media.

## Capital Eye

The Center also publishes a bimonthly newsletter, *Capital Eye*, which chronicles the latest trends and happenings in campaign finance at both the federal and state level. Call the Center at 202-857-0044 for a free subscription.

The Center is also available to work with news organizations and individual reporters on all aspects of campaign financing, from help in deciphering candidates' reports to assistance in setting up in-house databases. For a full list of other Center publications and reports, phone 202-857-0044 or write:

Center for Responsive Politics
1320 19th St. NW
Suite 700
Washington, DC 20036

# INDEX

# FEEDBACK

Consider this handbook version 1.0. It's certainly not a *complete* guide to tracking money and politics, nor will it ever be. But it can definitely improve, and it will. To be most useful, this book needs to grow in the right directions. Tell us what those directions are. Please fill out the following survey of what was useful, what you could live without, and what sections you'd like to see beefed up.

DON'T FILL THIS OUT UNTIL YOU'VE READ THE BOOK, or at least looked through it enough to figure out you'll never read it. You can even wait longer if you're using the book and testing its advice, BUT PLEASE SEND IN THE QUESTIONNAIRE.

Mail it to:
Center for Responsive Politics
1320 19th St. NW, Suite 700
Washington, DC 20036

Or fax it to us at 202-857-7809. Thanks!

*Which sections of the book did you read?*

| | | | | |
|---|---|---|---|---|
| I. The Money in the System | Whole thing | Some of it | Just a taste | Didn't read |
| II. Tracking the Money | Whole thing | Some of it | Just a taste | Didn't read |
| III. Reporting the Story | Whole thing | Some of it | Just a taste | Didn't read |
| Appendices | Whole thing | Some of it | Just a taste | Didn't read |

*How useful was each section?*

| | | | | |
|---|---|---|---|---|
| I. The Money in the System | Very useful | Useful | Sort of useful | Not useful |
| II. Tracking the Money | Very useful | Useful | Sort of useful | Not useful |
| III. Reporting the Story | Very useful | Useful | Sort of useful | Not useful |
| Appendices | Very useful | Useful | Sort of useful | Not useful |

*Which sections/chapters need expanding?*

_____

*Which sections/chapters could be cut?*

_____

*What did you like the most?*

_____

*What didn't you like?*

_____

*Do you plan to (circle all that apply)*

| | | | | |
|---|---|---|---|---|
| Download data from the FEC? | Yes | Might | Don't plan to | Already doing it |
| Start your own database? | Yes | Might | Don't plan to | Already doing it |

If you've done your own database, or plan to do one, what did you/will you put in your database and what political body or bodies does it cover (e.g., Montana legislature, part of Ohio State Senate, Baltimore City Council, etc.)?

_____

*If you're doing/planning your own database, is it . . . (circle as many as apply)*

Federal          State          Local

Would you be willing to share data with other states, in return for their data? _____

*Are you (mark all that apply) . . .*

Reporter ❏                    Student ❏
Editor ❏                      Academic ❏
TV/Radio Producer ❏          Other ❏
Other news executive ❏

How would you describe your . . .

| | | | |
|---|---|---|---|
| Familiarity with computers . . . | Experienced | New/light user | None |
| Familiarity with databases . . . | Experienced | New/light user | None |

| | | | |
|---|---|---|---|
| Do you work for a news organization? | | Yes | No |
| What media do you work in? Newspapers | Magazines | Radio | TV |

How did you get your copy of the FTM Handbook?

In the mail     Bought it     Co-worker     Other _____

*Optional:*

Name: _____

Organization: _____

Address: _____

City/State/Zip: _____

Phone: _____